GO IT ALONE

GO IT ALONE

THE SECRET TO BUILDING A SUCCESSFUL BUSINESS ON YOUR OWN

Bruce Judson

Collins

An Imprint of HarperCollinsPublishers

GO IT ALONE! © 2004 by Bruce Judson. All rights reserved.
Printed in the United States of America. No part of this book
may be used or reproduced in any manner whatsoever without
written permission except in the case of brief quotations
embodied in critical articles and reviews. For information,
address HarperCollins Publishers, 10 East 53rd Street, New
York, NY 10022.

HarperCollins books may be purchased for educational, business, or sales promotional use. For information, please write
to: Special Markets Department, HarperCollins Publishers, 10
East 53rd Street, New York, NY 10022.

First Collins edition published 2005.

Designed by Nancy Singer Olaguera

**The Library of Congress has catalogued the hardcover
edition as follows:**
Judson, Bruce.
    Go it alone! : the secret to building a successsful business
on your own / Bruce Judson.
        p. cm.
    Includes index.
    ISBN 0-06-073113-3
    1. New business enterprises—Management. 2. Entrepreneur-
ship. 3. Small business. I. Title.

HD62.5.J83   2004
658.1'141—dc22   2004052391

ISBN-13: 978-0-06-073114-4
ISBN-10: 0-06-073114-1

05 06 07 08 09 ❖ / RRD 10 9 8 7 6 5 4 3 2 1

This book is dedicated to
Mike Kitzmiller and the memory of Dana Meadows;
two people who have made a difference in my life.

ACKNOWLEDGMENTS

This book owes its existence to two people: Marion Maneker, my editor, and Robert Barnett, of Williams & Connolly in Washington, D.C. Marion Maneker is an editor's editor. It was an uplifting experience to work with someone who had an unwavering vision of what this book could be and helped me in every possible way to realize that potential. I am grateful to Bob Barnett, who represented me in this initiative, for his resolution to make this project happen.

I would also like to thank the four women in my life: my wife, Nancy, who was a source of unending encouragement and spent many hours enhancing the ideas in this book with her perceptive comments and questions; my daughter Emily, who never complained that Dad was less available for family activities during the several months it took to write this book; my daughter Rebekah, who brought her considerable sense of style to this manuscript; and my mother, Betty Judson, who imbued me with a lifelong fascination with the written word.

I am grateful, as well, to Jeff Garten, the dean of the Yale School of Management, and Stan Garstka, the school's deputy dean, for their support in the creation of this book. Edwin Tan of HarperBusiness also played a central role in bringing this book to fruition, for which I am thankful.

In interviews for this book, many people gave generously of their time and provided a wealth of thoughtful insights. I would like to extend my gratitude to this large and impressive group.

These individuals are acknowledged in the quotes and ideas attributed to them throughout this manuscript.

Finally, my father, the late Morris Judson, was the first person to encourage me—through words, deeds, and perseverance—to believe there was nothing a determined individual could not accomplish.

CONTENTS

INTRODUCTION

Conventional Wisdom Is Just Plain Wrong

The numbers are staggering.

Over half (56%) of all Americans dream of starting their own business. The United States is the land of opportunity, but so few of us ever make the leap to this fundamental aspiration. Work is a central part of our lives. Each week for 35 years or more—over 70,000 hours and often half of the time we are awake—most of us work (and travel to and from work). Yet, only a very few of us ever feel that we set our own course, work at what we do best, and are doing what we most love doing. Indeed, in late 2003, the Conference Board reported that U.S. job satisfaction hit a record low: Over half of all Americans are unhappy with their jobs. The Gallup Organization asked 1.7 million employees in 101 companies from 63 countries, "At work, do you have the opportunity to do what you do best every day?" Only 20% of the responding employees working at large firms answered yes. Finally, a 2004 Gallup poll found that over 70% of U.S. workers are "disengaged" from their jobs, meaning that almost three of every four workers have mentally checked out and lost any real commitment to their work or their company.

People are unhappy at work, can't use their unique skills, and want greater control of their destiny. Even more important, they feel they're wasting an important part of their lives. As Bob Fuhrer, a successful entrepreneur and the president of Nextoy, LLC, said, "When I was a kid working as a gofer, it was the older guys in the office whom you would always hear saying, 'I wish that at some point I had tried to make it on my own.' I was determined that when I was their age, I would not have this same regret."

When asked, "Well, why don't you start your own business?" people most often give reasons related to money. People stay at their jobs because they're worried about not being able to meet existing financial commitments. They believe that they don't have the financial resources required to successfully start their own businesses. These are certainly important and valid issues, but they no longer have to be the driving force in business life.

Today, the conventional wisdom about how to start a substantial business is just plain wrong. Now, you don't need to raise a lot of money first, you don't need a team of employees, and you don't need limitless financial resources. This book details how in today's business environment it is easier, and more possible, than ever to build a significant business on your own with no employees.

An important related issue is the perception of extraordinary high risk generally associated with starting your own venture. In all likelihood, almost all of the 56% of Americans (you or the person sitting next to you) who would like to be their own boss are aware of the high failure rate often cited for start-ups. The generally accepted rule of thumb is that 40% of new businesses die within the first year, and that over 80% of start-ups fail within the first five years. With widely reported odds like that, it's no wonder that people with ongoing financial responsibilities stay put.

This book, however, is also about how to dramatically limit the risk of failure associated with any new venture. You can substantially limit that risk. You can both avoid the mistakes that frequently lead to rapid business destruction and learn the steps that successful entrepreneurs take to avoid failures.

You can never completely eliminate risk. Indeed, life is filled with different kinds of risks. The first time we cross the street alone as youngsters, we're taught to limit the risk of being hit by a car by looking both ways before we start out. Starting a business is no different: By taking specific steps before you launch a business, you can increase your chances of success dramatically. It is now far easier to ensure that when you go it alone, you successfully cross the street the first time on your own.

Similarly, you can take specific steps to ensure that in this extraordinarily difficult, competitive climate, your business survives and thrives. This book details and demonstrates these ideas and strategies.

Starting your own business still requires hard work, dedication, and perseverance. In today's hypercompetitive environment it is impossible to suggest otherwise. The approach detailed here requires energy, determination, and discipline. But you'll hear from successful entrepreneurs here who consistently say that the freedom of working on your own makes it all worthwhile. They also find that this freedom brings them higher energy and greater focus: When you're on your own, you know that you're capturing the full value of your work. If you work hard, you're the one who reaps the rewards. When you accomplish something, you get the financial rewards and you have the satisfaction of knowing that you're the one benefiting from your efforts.

Finally, an important message of this book is that over the past few years, changes in the way businesses work and in supporting technology mean that there has never been a better time to start your own business. This book details how to conceptualize your business and how to focus your energy and efforts so that you can successfully go it alone.

THE POWER OF INDIVIDUALS

In part, this book is about the tremendous power of each individual. Americans rarely believe that people can accomplish great things in business on their own. As corporations grow ever larger, the conventional wisdom holds that the potential influence of solo entrepreneurs similarly diminishes. But in fact, the opposite can also be true. Individuals are now more powerful than ever.

This new power may not be entirely good: In ancient times, how much damage could any single person inflict on a group of people? With a stone, a stick, or a sword, one person couldn't harm too many others. With the invention of the machine gun and bombs, this power expanded. Today, we are all painfully aware that an individual terrorist could potentially use minia- ture nuclear weapons or biotechnology to harm large numbers of people. As our society has evolved, technology has empow- ered the individual.

This same empowerment in business today can have far- reaching effects. It is now possible for individuals, in a positive sense, to be "dangerous" in business. Oscar Wilde said that "an idea that is not dangerous is unworthy of being called an idea at all." This book is filled with ideas about how you can become positively dan- gerous in the business world when you go it alone.

WHO SHOULD READ THIS BOOK

This book is for anyone who has ever dreamed of owning his or her own business. Whether you consider that idea a vague yearning, a dream you hope to realize, or a necessity, this book's message is for you.

As a society, we have been led astray—to believe that to start a successful business you need to raise a great deal of money, take enormous risks, and recognize that the odds are you will fail anyway. That is just plain wrong, and this book explains why.

This book is for the one of every two Americans who dream of going out on their own, including:

- **Current and former corporate executives and employ- ees** who are seeking both greater financial rewards and greater control over their lives

- **Anyone who has recently lost his or her job** as a result of layoffs and is deciding what it makes sense to do next
- **Entrepreneurs** who will benefit from the innovative approaches suggested here
- **Small-business employees** who dream of starting their own enterprises but lack the capital
- **Stay-at-home parents** who want to reenter the workforce on their terms
- **Seniors** who want to create their own home business with control over their hours, one that takes advantage of their available time, not their capital

THE STORY BEHIND THIS BOOK

It's useful to understand how this book came about. In many ways, it represents the culmination of a multiyear odyssey that began at the Yale School of Management. Several years ago, I was coteaching a marketing course that involved the use of new Internet technologies. As I thought more and more about the implications of our subject—and interacted with colleagues and students—I became increasingly convinced that I was developing a new body of ideas related to starting a solo business. I found these ideas so compelling—and so counter to conventional wisdom—that I ultimately decided that there was only one thing to do: test my growing convictions by launching businesses of my own.

On the one hand, I conceived of these businesses as a living laboratory: They were to be a battle test of my seemingly heretical notions. On the other hand, I was also excited by the idea of starting substantial businesses that would let me be captain of my own fate and generate a valuable income for my family.

To date, I have started several businesses based on these ideas. One of these, Speed Anywhere, Inc. (www.SpeedAnywhere.com), is discussed at length in this book. The principal result of these efforts is my absolute conclusion that in appropriate circumstances, the ideas in this book have substantial merit. At the height of the telecommunications collapse, I launched what quickly became one of the nation's largest business-to-business broadband marketing firms. While the telecommunications industry lost 500,000 jobs and announced spectacular bankruptcies, I launched the business with almost no start-up capital, achieved profitability quickly, and served over 15,000 customers. For most of its life, Speed Anywhere has relied entirely on one part-time employee: me.

The results of my next business, Health Plans Today (www .HealthPlansToday.com), further added to my confidence in the ideas contained here. Within a month of its launch, I was one of the leading marketers of health insurance services on the Web. Today, over 2,500 different individuals and companies, both large and small, market health insurance services on the Web. My business quickly reached the top ranks of this overcrowded, extremely competitive market.

As the idea for this book took hold, I added a third leg to the support that then consisted of my ideas and my real-life experiences: I located and interviewed a large number of entrepreneurs who had similarly built substantial businesses with few or no employees and limited start-up capital. This research both expanded and confirmed my evolving ideas: These entrepreneurs expressed ideas that paralleled my own. In diverse industries, they employed similar operating principles and had surprisingly similar experiences. In this book, you'll meet many of these people. You'll see that they have all developed their different businesses according to some remarkably uniform ideas and approaches.

With this wealth of data and experience, it's time to debunk myths and demonstrate that a new age of entrepreneurship has begun.

1

OVERVIEW: THE NEW GO-IT-ALONE BUSINESS

THE EMERGENCE OF THE GO-IT-ALONE ENTREPRENEUR

A fundamentally new class of entrepreneur is emerging: the go-it-alone entrepreneur. Businesses run by these entrepreneurs are characterized by three defining criteria:

- The business is started with a minimal investment, and the founder or founders retain full ownership and control of the enterprise.
- The business is run entirely by a small number of people, generally from one to six.
- The founder does not set out to create a small business. He or she is working from the premise that the business has unlimited revenue potential.

To the founder or founders, a go-it-alone enterprise is small only in the numbers of workers it employs. It's designed to generate substantial financial returns and to play a sizable role in the business world.

The implications of these defining criteria are significant. When a business starts with a minimal investment, the enterprise must focus on generating cash from the outset. This, in turn, suggests that the business is able to swiftly develop a paying customer base. Unlike many start-ups, go-it-alone businesses don't have a gestation period where dedicated, full-time employees spend months developing plans and products.

Additionally, *go-it-alone business* is not simply a fancy term for a free agent or a freelancer. These businesses provide their founders with far more stability than freelance work and more personal rewards than franchising. These entrepreneurs are building a substantial asset. They have control of their own destiny. In difficult economic times, free agents and freelancers are typically in the extraordinarily frustrating position of waiting for the phone to ring. In contrast, go-it-alone entrepreneurs always a have focus for their energies and an asset that will provide them with an income stream.

Moreover, freelancers, free agents, and many small-business owners typically work on an hourly or daily rate, or they charge by the job. In all of these cases, they depend entirely on what they can produce as individuals, and their earnings are tied to the clock. They have not established a business system that allows them to magnify or leverage their skills. As a consequence, their earnings are inherently limited. Go-it-alone businesses don't suffer from this income constraint.

It's equally important to recognize that go-it-alone businesses can be started by almost anyone working in almost any sector of the economy:

- **Go-it-alone businesses are created by all types of people.** They are not limited to young people with nothing to lose, masters of the Internet, or sophisticated former corporate executives. They include women, former corporate employees of all kinds, seniors starting newly independent careers, people of all nationalities, stay-at-home parents who are rejoining the workforce, and individuals of all types and all ages who are pursuing their passion, realizing greater financial rewards, and achieving far greater control of their lives.
- **Go-it-alone enterprises create a wide range of products**

and services for businesses and consumers, as demonstrated by the examples and case studies in this book.

Successful go-it-alone businesses are not haphazard undertakings. If a go-it-alone business were a house, we would say that it was built on a well-constructed foundation, using a blueprint that involves several core engineering ideas. The ideas that form this foundation are discussed next.

THE IDEA OF PERSONAL LEVERAGE

Give me a lever and a place to stand and I will move the world.
—*Archimedes*

Achieving leverage and the amplification of your skills is the keystone to becoming a successful go-it-alone entrepreneur. A Roman arch cannot exist without its keystone. Similarly, an entrepreneur can turn his or her unique skills into a keystone that holds together a variety of outsourced services. Thus, a substantial go-it-alone business depends on the effective application of leverage and extreme outsourcing. The impact of one or a few people's talents can now be magnified through the combination of these two factors to an extent that was inconceivable even a few short years ago.

One simple example of the kind of leverage that exists today is generally evident in any Internet-based retailing effort:

- In the past, some of the functions required of any potential store proprietor included renting physical space, designing and furnishing the store, staffing the store during all hours of operations, and attracting walk-in traffic to the store through local advertising and other means. All of these activities took time, a substantial upfront cash investment, and multiple employees—leading to a substantial start-up cost and substantial operating expenses.

- In contrast, powerful, easy-to-use tools now make it possible for anyone with an idea for a store in the online world to get up and going at almost no cost—in a matter of hours. The Yahoo! Store, for example, typically charges under $100 per month and provides a full e-commerce suite. In the virtual world, unlike the physical world, stores are generally leased on a month-to-month basis: No large financial commitment to a multiyear lease is required.

That is not to suggest that Internet retailing is always a good business or even that it is an easy business. In fact, it can be an intensely competitive and often difficult business. The point is that in the past, it was not possible for a single person without access to capital to even consider participating in the business arena. Until recently, you either had to risk a great deal of money and time—if you could afford both—to start your own retail business or had to remain an employee somewhere. Today, the cost and time involved in becoming your own boss has decreased dramatically.

The risk of striking out on your own today can also be significantly decreased. Now, a person with a skill, a strong service idea, or an innovative product idea can achieve leverage through a wide range of inexpensive, easy-to-use services. The costs and time involved in getting a new business off the ground are substantially lower, which in turn makes such an effort a far less risky undertaking.

In this new working environment, the individual stands at the center of a carefully constructed business system. In Archimedes' world, physical power was amplified by combining a lever with a fulcrum. In today's world, business strength is achieved when you become the fulcrum, and the business system that you establish is the lever. It is now possible to amplify your own power by creating an effective business system.

For example, my company, Speed Anywhere, operates a fully automated system for channeling potential prospects for broadband to large telecommunications companies that will follow up with dedicated sales efforts. As a consequence, the vast majority of my time and energy concentrates on my marketing activities. And the total business system leverages these activities. If I implement an idea that cost-effectively doubles the number of prospects generated, everything else simply flows through the automated system with minimal increases in cost and no delays in time or efficiency.

DO WHAT YOU DO BEST—LET OTHERS DO THE REST

The idea of the virtual corporation is a myth. The idea of the extraordinarily focused business is the important reality.

Every successful go-it-alone entrepreneur has a very real skill that can range from an expertise in Internet marketing, to a graphic-arts capability, to a gift as a high-energy entertainer, to an expertise in using specific software, to a mechanical orientation, to a talent for routinizing complex activities. What distinguishes all of these businesses is that the founders have figured out a way to focus their efforts almost entirely around their individual skills—around what they do best. These owners have outsourced all other business functions to people who can provide them better or more cost effectively.

In *The 80/20 Principle: The Secret to Success by Achieving More with Less*, Richard Koch persuasively argues that most of us "only make good use of 20 percent of our time." The remaining 80% is typically spent on activities that make little difference to our overall success. Similarly, in *Now, Discover Your Strengths*, Marcus Buckingham and Donald Clifton studied the results of over one million Gallup poll interviews related to job activities and found that "the real tragedy in life is not that each of us doesn't have enough strengths, it's that we fail to use the ones we have." In contrast, successful go-it-alone entrepreneurs have figured out how to structure their businesses as systems that allow them to spend far more of their time on the meaningful, productive activities that take advantage of their greatest strengths. In Koch's terminology, they are able to significantly "move the time spent on high-value activities up from 20 percent."

The best way to describe this systematic approach is *extreme outsourcing*. Here, *outsourcing* does not mean sending jobs or functions out of the country (the practice of offshoring). It simply means that a specific function is handled not by the entrepreneur's business but a separate business. *Extreme* outsourcing is farming out absolutely everything except the core functions, which are designed to capitalize on your greatest strengths. Today, this type of outsourcing is easier than ever because of the Internet's communications capabilities, creating the instant exchange of information between separate companies that can be physically located thousands of miles apart.

Quite simply, innovative go-it-alone entrepreneurs employ extreme outsourcing because they recognize that their most valuable asset is their time, which allows them to achieve an unprecedented degree of focus. They know that they may be capable of doing many things, but they are constantly setting priorities that will best build their businesses. Go-it-alone entrepreneurs may be superb computer programmers, salespeople, or graphic artists, but they won't hesitate to outsource these functions if another entity can perform them well and cost-effectively. As much as possible, these entrepreneurs spend their time using the unique skills that make their businesses valuable.

A typical classic entrepreneur might say, "Yes, I can grow my business on my own—if I can only find 300 hours in each week." By outsourcing all the noncore functions of the business, the go-it-alone entrepreneur effectively creates those 300 hours a week!

John Maxwell, a leading authority on leadership, addresses the value of focus from a different perspective. In *Thinking for a Change: 11 Ways Highly Successful People Approach Life and Work*, he discusses research that has demonstrated that simply having too many tasks, even if you have the time to do them all, is a distraction that can radically decrease your effectiveness. "Switching from task to task can cost up to 40 percent efficiency," he notes. To create a working system that allows you to focus, you must create free time by limiting the sheer volume of different things to be done. Go-it-alone entrepreneurs do this through extreme outsourcing. In contrast, the vast majority of traditional solo entrepreneurs will tell you that they administer everything. They are the chief cook and bottle washer, as well as the CEO. The importance of this distinction cannot be underestimated.

Extreme outsourcing is, of course, closely related to personal leverage, discussed earlier. Indeed, they are the flip sides of the same coin. Go-it-alone entrepreneurs stand at the center of a highly focused business system, and their activities can be leveraged to provide extraordinary returns.

RELENTLESS REPEATABILITY: THE KEY TO LEVERAGING YOUR BUSINESS

To succeed, your business must do something that is repeatable. In *Beyond the Core: Expand Your Market Without Abandoning Your Roots*, Chris Zook borrows a well-known phrase from golf legend Ben Hogan, "relentless repeatability." Hogan described this ability as the secret to his extraordinary success. As Zook notes, "it is an apt term for one of the most critical elements in the growth of companies, the discovery of a repeatable formula to drive profitable growth."

Similarly, there is a well-known adage that is often repeated to people who are launching business consulting ventures: Until you have generated at least one client that you did not know before you started consulting, you have not succeeded. The point here is that it is easiest to build on pre-existing relationships and sell services to people you already know. But ultimately, you will exhaust this pool. To thrive, you need a mechanism for repeatedly selling your services to a broader pool of clients.

The essence of a repeatable business is the ability to create processes and systems that determine exactly how the business will work. Here's a useful test: Is it possible to write in a notebook all of the information on how your prospective business will work? If so, then you have created a repeatable system. I am not suggesting that you undertake such a time-consuming exercise. I am, however, saying that you only have a repeatable formula when you have simplified and routinized your activities to the point that such a manual could be created.

To apply the concepts of leverage and extreme outsourcing discussed earlier, you need a repeatable formula. It's the formula that determines which ingredients of your business should be outsourced and leveraged. A case study at the beginning of Chapter 5, pages 106–108, shows how these concepts can be applied to create a winning business and demonstrates that you can create a repeatable formula for almost any kind of activity.

GOOD IDEAS ARE EVERYWHERE

Sometimes people assume that the key to entrepreneurial success is finding that one incredibly good idea. This suggests that there is a shortage of good business ideas. But in fact, one of the central findings of my ongoing research is that there is an abundance of good ideas. As detailed in Chapter 3, "The Great Shift in What's Possible," the rapid changes occurring in the way business works are daily creating more and more opportunities for go-it-alone entrepreneurs.

Where do good business ideas originate?

The answer turns out to be far simpler than most people imagine. Over and over again, successful go-it-alone entrepreneurs find their inspiration in solutions they developed for their own real-life problems. They typically encounter a problem, solve it for themselves, and then conclude that "if I needed this, other people probably do as well."

Mr. Trademark (www.MrTrademark.com), which provides online trademark searches and related services, is one example that illustrates this point. Joe Strahl, the founder of this business, was formerly the owner of *Prison Life* magazine. When copyright issues related to the magazine arose, Strahl found that rather than pay a lawyer, he could research existing trademarks for free through a database that was available at the New York Public Library. After completing this work, Strahl realized that the basic research to determine the existence of any trademark conflicts does not require a lawyer. He concluded that he could build a profitable business around this research service. The benefits Mr. Trademark offers include far lower costs than those of lawyer-guided trademark investigation services and guaranteed 24-hour turnaround.

Mr. Trademark's beginning is far more the norm than the exception. In fact, the *majority* of the go-it-alone businesses described here started the same way: The founder solved a problem in his or her own life.

I often find myself in situations where people are discussing good ideas for start-up businesses. These days, I participate by asking one simple question with two missing words: "In the past few weeks, when have you said to yourself, 'I wish that there was a _____ so that I would not have to _____,' and how did you solve this problem?" The answer is often the basis for a strong go-it-alone business idea.

2

PRINCIPLES FOR SUCCESS

Go-it-alone entrepreneurs have carefully thought through the dynamics of their business system and eliminated the potential bottlenecks to growth. With few exceptions, these businesses share several core operating principles: These stand at the heart of every successful go-it-alone business. We've already discussed three of these: personal leverage, extreme outsourcing, and relentless repeatability, that enable founders to focus on what they do best. The remaining 10 principles, listed below, are discussed at length in this chapter:

- Focus on reducing the risks associated with a potential failure.
- Never get too far ahead of your customers.
- Make a rigorous commitment to flexibility and ongoing innovation.
- Create the ability to scale.
- Maintain an experimental attitude.
- Take yourself off the clock.
- Master the potential of new technologies.
- Develop a bias toward action, starting with small steps.
- Affirm your determination—make a commitment to find a way.
- Only use off-the-shelf products and services.

FOCUS ON REDUCING THE RISKS ASSOCIATED WITH A POTENTIAL FAILURE

There tends to be a general belief that entrepreneurs are somewhat like Don Quixote: They fearlessly go forward, at tremendous peril to themselves and in the face of overwhelming odds. In fact, the idea of the entrepreneur as a bold, swashbuckling risk-taker is a modern myth. Yes, there are flamboyant entrepreneurs who may repeatedly risk everything, but they are the exceptions, not the rule. In general, today's successful entrepreneurs are a surprising mix of prudence and courage: They aren't afraid to try new things, but they first do everything they can to reduce all costs and risks.

Go-it-alone entrepreneurs are optimistic but realistic. Though they recognize that risk is an essential part of business, they are constantly asking themselves, "Now how can I limit the damage if this does not work?" By limiting their risk, they work to ensure they will still be in business even if a particular initiative doesn't work.

In March 2001, eMachines (www.eMachines.com) was in dire straits, and Wayne Inouye was hired as the new CEO. Most analysts assumed that Inouye would head straight for bankruptcy court. Instead, Inouye engineered one of the most stunning turnarounds in recent memory. After eMachines overtook Gateway (www.Gateway.com) to become the nation's third largest desktop PC company, the two companies chose to merge, with Inouye becoming CEO of the combined company.

Inouye echoes this generally unrecognized aspect of successful entrepreneurs: "We are used to thinking of entrepreneurs as people who embrace tremendous risk. In my experience, successful entrepreneurs do everything they can to limit risk. They may take a risk on a new business model or a concept that has not been tried before—and they are not afraid of risk, but within that framework, they do everything they can to limit the costs of failure."

Go-it-alone entrepreneurs actively manage risk. Indeed, it's common for them to find a way to test the validity of their business idea before making it a full-time effort. As we will see, a surprising number of successful go-it-alone entrepreneurs start businesses in their spare time before they quit their day jobs.

For example, Niveus Media (www.NiveusMedia.com) produces an all-in-one low-priced entertainment PC that combines the power of a computer with the functionality of a digital video recorder (DVR), a DVD player, and an MP3 jukebox that has received rave reviews. The company's innovative business model was lauded in *Business 2.0* magazine. Nonetheless, Tim Cutting, Niveus Media's CEO, is happy to point out to that he and his two partners built their entire business at night and on weekends while maintaining their existing jobs. At the time the *Business 2.0* article was published, Cutting was an employee at Sun Microsystems.

What's particularly relevant here is that by maintaining their day jobs, Tim Cutting and his partners dramatically reduced the risk associated with starting their own firm. With a new baby in the house, he wanted to pursue his dream of starting a new business but did not want to put financial pressure on the business to yield instant profits. And, as he said, "What if despite all of the best-laid plans, we discovered a flaw in the business?" By starting it in their spare time, Cutting and his partners got the business off the ground with minimal personal risks.

The story of Tim Cutting and his partners illustrates two important tactics of go-it-alone entrepreneurs: While they are still refining their business concept (1) they reduce risk by gaining as much experience as possible with paying customers, and (2) they avoid putting pressure on the business for fast financial success by keeping their day jobs.

The high value of working with actual customers—as opposed to relying on market research—is particularly noteworthy in light of with a well-publicized business failure that occurred last winter. MedImmune, a Maryland-based biotechnology company, developed FluMist, a flu vaccine that is administered as a nasal spray rather than a potentially painful shot. The company and Wythe, the comarketer of the nasal spray, forecast sales of four million to six million doses in the first year. This seemed possible, since 60 million to 90 million Americans receive shots annually.

Unfortunately, actual sales were far below these expectations; the rollout was a failure. The *New York Times* reported that the company acted on flawed information that executives said "our market research led us to believe." FluMist was positioned as a premium product, with a price of $49 per dose, several times higher than a flu shot. In contrast to the predictions generated from market research, it turned out that consumers preferred the pain of the shot, as opposed to paying extra for the nasal spray.

This failure, as well as countless others, vividly illustrates that market research is never as valuable as actual experience with paying customers. People will say they'll take a particular action, but what they actually do—when real expenses are involved—can turn out to be quite different. Innovators commonly assume that their products or services will quickly command an unrealistically high price. As a member of the board of directors of multiple start-ups, I've seen this phenomenon over and over again. The formal business plan—with supporting data—assumes that customers will, for example, jump to pay $29.95 for a product. But when the launch occurs, the firm discovers building a substantial customer base makes a far lower price necessary. Whatever the cause of these miscalculations, successful go-it-alone entrepreneurs do absolutely everything possible in advance to work with real customers to avoid these mistakes.

The second risk-reducing tactic is also evident in the founding of Niveus Media. More often than not, businesses don't succeed as rapidly as the founders anticipate. Indeed, the history of new businesses is filled with stories of companies of now-legendary success that were close to closing their doors because sales materialized far slower than anticipated. By testing business concepts at night and on weekends, go-it-alone entrepreneurs can significantly enhance their ultimate chances of success.

Successful entrepreneurs recognize that there is no such thing as a sure thing, so they work to reduce the possibility of failure before they launch their companies and to give themselves plenty of time to build the business. One business founder describes this operating philosophy succinctly: "You never know what problems you may encounter until you actually try. And some of these problems may be deal-breakers. You need to find a low-cost way to get out there and see what works."

NEVER GET TOO FAR AHEAD OF YOUR CUSTOMERS

Some in the business community are obsessed with the idea that successful new businesses are inherently revolutionary. This false conception can cripple a start-up.

Why is this belief so strong? We tend to look at the greatest entrepreneurs—after they have worked for years to succeed—and focus on the net result of their efforts. A successful start-up *may* reinvent a business—but not overnight. We look at a business's total accomplishments and see only the revolution it created. We don't recognize how the company may have slowly nurtured change among its customers over many years. Moreover, companies that revolutionize industries are, by their nature, the most likely to receive attention in the press. They are interesting and newsworthy. But the skewed volume of coverage devoted to these firms contributes to the myth that these dramatic innovators are the rule and not the exception.

Products and services sell when they are just new enough to fulfill an unmet customer need without reinventing every other aspect of the customer's life; *revolutionary services rarely do.* Because they are so innovative, revolutionary services typically suffer from a slow pace of adoption, meaning that many fail because they take too much time to generate cash.

Rosabeth Moss Kanter, a professor at the Harvard Business School, expressed this same idea, in an article in *Business 2.0*: "The path to success involves staying a little ahead of the competition but close enough that customers can understand your product and incorporate it into their lives and businesses." Kanter extensively studied the reasons some companies succeed and others do not. Her conclusion: "Years of research shows that the innovations most likely to take hold are those that don't demand excessive change from the customer."

This truth was vividly brought home to me in a discussion I had with Dr. Ross Jaffe, one of the nation's leading health care venture capitalists. Jaffe, a managing director at Versant Ventures based in Menlo Park, California, was analyzing the business I had developed selling health insurance online, Health Plans Today. This business, which allows prospects to access a database of thousands of potential plans and compare offerings, is a pure use of my expertise in Web marketing.

Jaffe noted that although I might be employing some innovative techniques, I was actually just a new kind of middleman in an industry that was accustomed to working with intermediaries. The business might operate in the online medium, but, Jaffe said, "Health insurance companies accepted long ago that they would need to work through brokers because consumers wanted to compare different options. You may have figured out the Internet equivalent of this activity, but from the perspective of a health insurance company or the consumer, it's not a dramatic change." *And he was right.*

Jaffe made one additional, critical point. He noted that "in health care, we see terrific plans to reform the entire system every week. Entrepreneurs bring us business plans describing software systems that could allow insurers, patients, and providers to communicate online, perhaps eliminate billions of dollars in waste, and improve the lives of everyone concerned. Unfortunately, to date, none of these businesses have worked." Jaffe concluded that "they all required too much change on the part of all of the buyers and sellers in the system, and no new business has the time or staying power to create that kind of change in order to build its market."

The significance of Jaffe's insight cannot be emphasized strongly enough. The U.S. Secretary of Health and Human Services estimates that if the health care delivery system incorporated information technology common in other industries, the United States would save over $100 billion a year. Indeed, this need has been recognized for decades, prompting a wave of start-ups that attempted to use the Internet to fix the health care system through improvements in information technology. Jaffe notes, however, that "despite raising hundreds of millions of dollars, these companies underestimated the inertia in the health care system and the resistance to adoption of new information technologies by health care providers and payers. They required too much new behavior on the part of the buyers of these systems, and most failed as businesses."

The lesson, again, is that to survive and thrive, go-it-alone entrepreneurs must build a paying customer base quickly. To do this, successful entrepreneurs focus on starting businesses that don't require dramatic shifts in the behavior of customers, suppliers, or service providers. Though such businesses *may* turn out to be revolutionary change agents, they typically start out as evolutionary improvements with a value that customers can see immediately.

MAKE A RIGOROUS COMMITMENT TO
FLEXIBILITY AND ONGOING INNOVATION

Several years ago Andy Grove, the well-known CEO of Intel, told us, with the title of his book, that *Only the Paranoid Survive*. There is no question that businesses today operate in an intensely competitive environment. The life cycle for new products is decreasing, and new opportunities arise and disappear with extraordinary speed. How can a solo entrepreneur hope to thrive over the long term?

Go-it-alone entrepreneurs achieve long-term success in part through an ongoing commitment to continuous low-cost innovation and to flexible business systems. By building their infrastructure through low-cost outsourced services that charge monthly subscription rates, these businesses can rapidly adapt to changes in the market and in their perceptions of opportunities.

Flexibility in Action

Peter Drucker is generally regarded as the father of modern management and the nation's preeminent business philosopher. He believes that it is almost impossible to predict exactly how a business will succeed. In a compendium of his work titled *The Essential Drucker*, he writes that "when a new venture does succeed, more often than not it is in a market other than the one it was originally intended to serve, with products or services not quite those with which it had set out, bought in large part by customers it did not even think of when it started."

To thrive amid this uncertainty, Drucker prescribes extraordinary flexibility and an absolute focus on the customer: "If a new venture does not anticipate this, organizing itself to take advantage of the unexpected and unseen markets: if it is not totally market-focused, if not market-driven, then it will succeed only in creating an opportunity for a competitor." In

Drucker's view, a new venture must be set up to capitalize on the inevitable unexpected opportunities and to avoid being hamstrung by an infrastructure designed to support the inevitable failed efforts. "Rather than dismiss the unexpected as an 'exception,' as entrepreneurs are inclined to do, they need to go out and look at it carefully and as a distinct opportunity."

Drucker's notion can be expanded to incorporate the idea that almost nothing succeeds in its first incarnation. Typically, a business prospers through a continuing loop of effort, assessment of results, and modifications based on learning. This process is very much within Drucker's admonition to be market-focused, if not market-driven.

Successful go-it-alone entrepreneurs expect and plan for the possibility that their initial market targeting may be wrong, and for continuous learning. Here are some examples:

- Gourmet Gatherings (http://GourmetGatherings.com), a highly successful San Francisco–based culinary entertainment company that now specializes in corporate team-building events, private cooking parties, and social events. The company was launched with the belief that "we would primarily be creating parties for individuals," says Shannan Bishop, one of the two founding partners. In fact, over 60% of the firm's business now comes from the corporate market, which has very different needs and requirements.
- Emoonlighter.com, now Guru.com (www.Guru.com), was launched as a marketplace for individuals with full-time jobs seeking part-time evening and weekend work. However, it succeeded as a marketplace for contract workers pursuing full-time projects.
- Speed Anywhere was launched as a consumer-oriented broadband marketer. Yet, the business succeeded only after it became a business-to-business marketer.

Go-it-alone businesses are total systems that by necessity are designed with the maximum possible flexibility. As a result, they are created from a perspective that significant shifts in the product, the service, and the customer base will be necessary—and frequent.

Innovation in Action

The continuous launching of new products and services is a notion to which almost every business pays lip service. But go-it-alone businesses really do it. The owners talk to you about what they have done to improve their offerings over the past month, and the specific timetable for ongoing releases over the next month. They also tell you that an enormous percentage of their time is focused on developing and implementing their next offering. Indeed, this systematic approach is a central way that solo entrepreneurs manage and reduce their risk. They clearly understand that in our fast-changing world, it's best to have your eggs in more than one potentially vulnerable basket.

Moreover, successful go-it-alone entrepreneurs have figured out how to test and launch new products and services quickly and at minimal cost. Although there is no single answer as to how they accomplish this objective, they all put a great deal of time and effort into mastering this art. As part of this process, they develop specific metrics for judging whether they have a winner or a loser.

Here are some examples of different approaches to the need for low-cost product testing and introduction:

- Lars Hundley, the founder of CleanAirGardening.com—an online environmentally friendly gardening store—operates a go-it-alone business through extreme outsourcing: He is the only employee. He finds that "no matter how good I think a product looks, I never know if it will actually sell on the Web. It may be that for some reason I don't realize buyers want to see and touch it. Or I may not realize that a version of the product is already available in every corner store." Hundley uses a dual testing technique. First, he tests sales of the products on eBay. If the product does not even fetch his wholesale cost, he knows he has a loser. On the other hand, products may sell on eBay for more than his anticipated retail price, which is the first encouraging news. Once a product survives the eBay test, he will buy a few items from the wholesaler and test sales on his Web site. If they perform according to his predetermined metrics, he will make a larger commitment to the product. If not, he is likely to drop it.

- At Speed Anywhere, I quickly realized that a key to marketing was product segmentation: I wanted buyers to recognize that a specific site could absolutely meet their needs. So I went from general broadband business lines, such as T1 Anywhere (www.T1Anywhere.com) (a T1 is a basic business broadband connection) to more specialized offerings such as private lines, offered through Private Line Anywhere (www.PrivateLine Anywhere.com). From the beginning, I consciously designed my business systems with enormous flexibility. Because of that, and with experience, I could launch a new service at almost no cost in under 4 hours. I also developed some proprietary targeted advertising techniques, using search engines, that allowed me to see how prospects responded to the site—and estimate its overall potential—for less than $50. In essence, I created a mechanism to continuously expand my product line with a minimal dollar investment and a relatively small investment of my time.

- Joe Strahl, the founder of Mr. Trademark, found himself in the fortunate but not uncommon position of working with customers who told him how he should expand his services. Strahl said: "We would finish a trademark search and then a customer would ask us if we offered other services such as trademark filing or preparing patent applications. I started to call this the 'do you do this phenomenon.' I always said sure. Then we would meet that commitment and in the process decide if this was a service we wanted to offer on a regular basis." Strahl's metrics required that any service offered on a regular basis by Mr. Trademark be largely automated and generate, on average, a specific profit number for every 15-minute period allocated to serving a client.

Mr. Trademark's approach is noteworthy for two reasons: It's one clear demonstration of how successful go-it-alone entrepreneurs also turn down paying business. By establishing clear profit objectives, Strahl could quickly assess whether specific activities were worthwhile. Unfortunately, many start-up businesses are seduced by the lure of revenues without clearly assessing the profitability associated with these revenues. It also demonstrates how customers are often the best source of new product ideas. Unsolicited customer requests for related new services are a recurring theme for go-it-alone entrepreneurs. This is one of the many reasons the most successful solo entrepreneurs work extra hard to stay in close touch with their customers.

The mantra for each of the businesses discussed above could easily be the same: They develop a quick, inexpensive process for discovering what new products and services potential customers will buy. The benefits here are threefold: (1) They rarely waste precious dollars on failed launches, (2) They limit the time they devote to any unsuccessful initiative, and (3) They view their business as a constantly evolving, flexible system that can maintain its competitive edge.

CREATE THE ABILITY TO SCALE

If growth can be managed without adding employees or new complexity, then there are effectively no limits to what one individual or a small number of people can accomplish: Go-it-alone entrepreneurs have figured out precisely how to accomplish this. In the wide range of industries in which they operate, these entrepreneurs have developed simple business systems that magnify their skills and allow their businesses to scale. In many cases, it's almost hard to imagine that businesses of such significant sizes are run entirely by solo entrepreneurs.

In fact, there is nothing mysterious about how these entrepreneurs create businesses that scale. The business systems involved are discussed in detail later in this book. It's important to point out, though, that these businesses can grow precisely because the founders have spent a great deal of their energy thinking through exactly how the business will operate. One book of tremendous value to any start-up entrepreneur that addresses this issue is *The E-Myth Revisited: Why Most Small Businesses Don't Work and What to Do About It*, by Michael Gerber. As Gerber forcefully demonstrates, a substantial portion of the founder's time must be spent working *on* the business, not *in* the business.

MAINTAIN AN EXPERIMENTAL ATTITUDE

If you ask what businesses will, in all likelihood, succeed or fail in the next 18 months, there is only one sure answer: Those that are still doing things today the way they did 18 months ago are far more likely to have failed.

We live in a world of extreme competition. With instant communication and the Internet, we no longer compete against other providers or suppliers in our neighborhood, our city, or even our state. Often, we are literally competing with people and entities on the other side of the country or even around the world. What does this mean?

First, it means that you must assume that if you are a success, others have noticed what you are doing and will copy you. One leading inventor said that "the most difficult thing is simply knowing that something can be done." Once this individual saw that something *could* be done, he knew that with enough effort he could eventually figure out *how* it was done. The knowledge that it had been done already told him that the particular problem in question could be solved. All businesspeople should take this to mean that competitors can—and are working—to reverse-engineer whatever they are doing.

Successful go-it-alone businesspeople are constantly in an experimental mode:

- Just as you want to design your business with the flexibility to shift your product mix, you also want to be constantly operating live tests of potential improvements in your core business. For me, this means that at any one moment I am conducting somewhere between 5 and 10 different tests of how services are marketed on the Web.
- You can, in part, measure whether you are living up to this goal by the time you devote to the process. My rule of thumb is that at least 1 hour a day should be devoted to creating and administering tests of new business initiatives.

An important point here is that an experimental attitude encompasses both ongoing curiosity and a willingness to constantly reconsider your business assumptions. Inder Guglani, the founder of Emoonlighter.com, now Guru.com, says that his firm tests, learns, and then constantly evaluates. His point is that the world has become such a dynamic place that "what works today at scale may not work tomorrow." So the firm must keep assessing how it functions. (See Chapter 5, pages 111–114, for a detailed discussion of how Guglani applied these principles to build a remarkably successful go-it-alone business.)

I have a close friend (who did not want his name to appear in this book) who operates a go-it-alone business that generates in excess of $1 million per year in profits. I estimate that he spends fully 50% of his time experimenting with ways to increase the effectiveness of the business. "You never know when a competitor will come in," he says. "The only way I can ensure that the business lasts is to keep developing new ways of operating."

In his influential book *Leading the Revolution: How to Thrive in Turbulent Times by Making Innovation a Way of Life*, Gary Hamel similarly argues that a portfolio of experiments is critical to the survival of enterprises: "Ask yourself if your company has a portfolio of . . . ongoing experiments. If it doesn't . . . its future is at risk." While Hamel is concerned with larger firms, the same basic reasoning holds true for smaller firms, which are inherently less stable. He notes that *all* experiments are valuable, regardless of outcome. "Most experiments won't pay off. But this hardly means they are worthless. . . . Every experiment produces learning, which . . . can help a company increase the odds that the next radical idea finds its mark."

TAKE YOURSELF OFF THE CLOCK

As go-it-alone entrepreneurs develop business ideas, they focus hard on *the idea of time*. The central question you want to constantly ask yourself is how you can get the greatest benefits out of the use of your time. In a practical sense, this means you want to look for business ideas that don't necessarily link your time to your compensation.

The clearest example of a time-dependent business is any kind of personal service. Doctors, lawyers, and counselors of all kinds earn incomes based on the time they spend with clients or patients. The leverage available to these types of businesses is limited. Nurses who help doctors make better use of their time are one form of leverage; so are paralegals who take care of the less complex aspects of a lawyer's activities.

The absolute contrast to a personal-service business is an automated business that earns money while you sleep. The ultimate example of a business of this kind is a digital book sold on the Internet. Here, your personal time does not limit your income potential. If you can create demand for this information product, an infinite number of customers can buy it (via an inexpensive Web site with an automated payment system) and receive it (through an easy-to-establish automated fulfillment system that sends a password or the digital content itself via e-mail to the buyer).

This is not to say that you should establish a digital book business. Rather, it is meant to illustrate the importance of time in assessing your business idea and operations. It's likely that you will develop a business that makes use of a mix of your time and leveraged systems: The important point is to recognize that the more you can create a product based income stream (such as a digital book), the higher your income potential—because you have eradicated the limits created when income is tied to time.

Here are some examples of businesses that have been designed, or shifted, to limit their time dependence:

- JangoMail (www.JangoMail.com) is a sophisticated e-mail management service provider for over 300 clients in 2004, including Nokia, Epson, Reuters, Wells Fargo, and General Motors. The company is profitable and has two full-time employees. Ajay Goel, the company's CEO, started the company specifically because he wanted to create a business that had "a recurring revenue stream and did not require constant selling to prospects and previous customers." He wanted a business that would leverage his time and talents.

It's noteworthy that the development of JangoMail reflects an evolution: In 1998, Goel started a successful Web development company that was quickly profitable. Over time, he saw that to grow in revenues and profitability, he needed to develop a different type of business: one that provided real value by continuously leveraging assets, not by charging for development or time. Goel's first attempt involved Internet content and was unsuccessful, but he was still determined to make the jump. The origin of JangoMail is one of many examples of the notion advanced earlier: that actual experiences with real problems are the best sources of new business ideas. During the course of a Web development project, Goel realized that there was a need for an e-mail management service that could easily tie into existing corporate e-mail databases—and that no such service existed. JangoMail was created to meet this need.

- Sherman Eisner's A&E Home Security Company (www .AESecurity.com) is a Web-based retailer of do-it-yourself home security systems. Eisner, who notes that he has always been mechanically inclined, believes that his unique strength is the ability to envision a customer's problems and walk them, over the phone, through solutions. Eisner has tied this skill to a retail business and has built a strong, nationwide presence. A central part of Eisner's success is that he can provide essential sales support and customer service over the phone without leaving the office, meaning that his time is highly leveraged. Moreover, his customers benefit from a pricing model that reflects self-installation, yet they can access his expertise in choosing and installing systems.

- Deborah Fischman owns Food and Balance (www.Foodand Balance.com), located in South Salem, New York. Fischman, who is also a full-time mother, was looking for a business endeavor she could operate from home that meshed with her family responsibilities, her passions, and her skills. She studied at the Institute for Integrative Nutrition in New York City and now provides counseling to people who "know they could feel and be healthier if they adopted different food and lifestyle choices." She started her business by providing clients with a 6-month program that included two individual sessions each month and one group cooking class.

  As she has been building her business, Fischman has started to focus on two factors: (1) Does she have something of continuing value that she can offer clients who have finished her 6-month program? (2) Can she leverage what's unique about her services in order to get more out of her time? Fischman's solution is worthy of note. She has found that her cooking classes serve multiple functions for clients: reinforce the goals developed in one-on-one sessions; provide attendees, who share common goals and interests, a support network; and provide a fun, social occasion.

  To leverage her time and create an ongoing income stream, Fischman is planning to offer clients who have finished her 6-month program the opportunity to pay a modest monthly fee in order to continue attending her cooking classes and receive other benefits (such as an e-mail newsletter with appropriate recipes and nutrition tips.) In effect, Fischman is now creating a hybrid business model: Her base business is highly time-dependent, but she is adding services that offer high value to her customers, are far more leveraged (as measured by her revenues per hour of work), and provide a means for her to increase her income.

The above discussion should not be interpreted to mean that service businesses are bad businesses. In fact, the personal contact typical of these businesses can be terrifically rewarding. Moreover, you may be able to create an income that meets your particular needs by offering a specific, repeatable service. The central point is, however, that a dependence on time does necessarily constrain your potential income. The income you can generate is limited by the hours you can bill.

MASTER THE POTENTIAL OF NEW TECHNOLOGIES

Most go-it-alone businesses would not have been possible even a few years ago. Some are Internet based; many others are not. But they all use new Internet-based service and communications to leverage their own efforts. Here are some illustrative cases:

- **Companies that are not Internet businesses use Internet services to leverage their time:** Gourmet Gatherings, the culinary entertainment company, uses inexpensive Internet-based services to coordinate assignments for its many events. Irwin Toy (www.IrwinToy.com) uses the Internet to work with designers across North America and make decisions about product modifications in real time. "In the past, to work with off-site designers was either impossible or we would have had to send materials back and forth by courier in a lengthy decision-making process," notes principal George Irwin. "Now, we are all simultaneously looking at the same images on the Web. We save enormous amounts of time and can make better decisions faster." (See Chapter 3, pages 74–77, for a description of Irwin's innovative go-it-alone toy business.)
- **Retailers take advantage of the opportunities created by new Internet technology:** In essence, the Internet allows

entrepreneurs to aggregate the entire nation into a small community. During the 2003 Christmas shopping season, the *New York Times* reported that the number-one seller in Amazon.com's specialty meat department was, at one point, elevages magret duck breast from Fossil Farms. The duck topped offerings from such well-known brands as Omaha Steaks. While there may not be enough people in any one geographic community with an interest in a specialty item, the Internet turns the entire world into a single shopping neighborhood. Lance Applebaum, Fossil's CEO, notes that the company is "a small business," but "Amazon (www.Amazon.com) lets us show off on a worldwide basis." Another example of Internet-based retailing, which simply was not possible a few years ago, is, of course, eBay (www.ebay.com). Over 400,000 people now report that eBay is their main source of income.

- **Enterprises take advantage of the phenomenon of unbundling, an inherent result of the Internet's growth:** For example, local telecommunications agents used to find, sell, and install lines in a specific geographic area. Now, these three functions are exploding apart. Speed Anywhere starts this chain of events by finding the prospects. The Internet makes seamless handoffs possible, so that all of these functions no longer have to operate under one roof. Instead, specialized businesses can do what they do best, and then pass their work on to the next specialized participant in the chain. Indeed, the significance for go-it-alone entrepreneurs of the accelerating trend toward such unbundling is explored at length in Chapter 3, pages 70–79.

To operate a go-it-alone business you do not, by any means, need to be a Web expert. As discussed at length in the next chapter, the essential Web services that make these businesses possible are becoming both more sophisticated and easier to use every day. You do, however, need to be willing to understand what these services can do to support your business, and to use them. Your competitors, in any arena, certainly will.

DEVELOP A BIAS TOWARD ACTION, STARTING WITH SMALL STEPS

A journey of a hundred miles begins with a single step.

—*Lao-tzu*

We are all familiar with people who are unsatisfied with their jobs and yearn to go out on their own. Many of them talk about starting a business—sometimes endlessly, without ever taking action. They see starting a business as an overwhelming, all-or-nothing task.

In contrast, go-it-alone entrepreneurs take the first steps, however small, to establish their business initiatives. Though it's a cliché that everything begins with a small first step, it's particularly true here. These entrepreneurs have figured out how to begin inventing their own business without completely abandoning their jobs or risking everything in one roll of the dice. This first step then leads to another and another, so that by the time these people have created a new business, they've often created a new life for themselves. This deliberate, incremental approach makes success much more likely.

In *The Power of Focus: How to Hit Your Business, Personal and Financial Targets with Absolute Certainty*, Jack Canfield, Mark Hansen, and Les Hewitt, describe the benefits of this approach to getting started:

Many people live their lives in ready-steady mode, instead of ready steady Go! You must go. Kickstart yourself into focused action. Just take the first step. Gradually you will build momentum. Like the proverbial snowball rolling downhill, you won't be able to stop after you make that early push. Remember, the big rewards in life only materialize when you start doing.

In *Start Small, Finish Big: Fifteen Key Lessons to Start—and Run—Your Own Successful Business,* Fred Deluca, the cofounder of Subway, writes with John Hayes. He similarly describes an action-oriented operating philosophy as central to the success of Subway. In a chapter, titled "Ready, Fire, Aim" he notes,

> . . . I prefer the philosophy of: Ready, Fire, Aim . . . especially when you're starting small. If you make a mistake, if you guess wrong, if your aim is off, you can fix it, and fire again, and adjust again, and again as needed.
>
> We used the Ready, Fire, Aim philosophy to start and grow Subway. When you're just getting started it's sometimes necessary to make a quick decision, take a shot, and then make course corrections as necessary. If you're willing to fire before you aim perfectly, you probably won't hit your target precisely, but you'll have taken that first step in the journey . . .

AFFIRM YOUR DETERMINATION—MAKE A COMMITMENT TO FIND A WAY

We will either find a way or make one.

—Hannibal

The one word that best characterizes successful entrepreneurs is *determination.* The act of creation from nothing is never easy. Nonetheless, the *will* to make something happen is an essential quality for a go-it-alone entrepreneur.

John Osher is widely recognized as one of the nation's most

successful entrepreneurs. He developed the Spin Pop, a spinning lollipop with a toy attached that was sold to Hasbro, for $120 million, and then developed the SpinBrush, a toothbrush that Procter & Gamble purchased for $475 million. He adopted *Determination* as his personal motto. Osher is widely quoted as saying that "if I were to write a book it would be called *Find A Way.*" In Osher's view, successful entrepreneurs will inevitably encounter obstacles but must somehow find a way around them. In an interview with *Entrepreneur* magazine, he enumerated the 17 most common mistakes entrepreneurs make, including the belief that something isn't possible: "If you're an entrepreneur, you're going to break new ground. A lot of people are going to say it's not possible. You can't accept that too easily. A good entrepreneur is going to find a way."

The analogy between business and warfare is often drawn. One classic discussion treatment of this idea, by marketing gurus Al Reiss and Jack Trout, is *Marketing Warfare*. I do not want to overstate such similarities here. Nonetheless, when it comes to the need for determination, the analogy is quite appropriate. Winston Churchill, Britain's embattled World War II leader said, "It is no use saying 'We are doing our best.' You have to succeed in doing what is necessary." The point that both Osher and Churchill are making is that in most cases in our personal and professional lives it's satisfactory to conclude, "I tried my hardest." In other cases, such as starting your own business, this is not sufficient: *You must be determined enough to find a way to succeed*. Here, there is no grade of A for effort.

Michael Moritz of Sequoia Capital, who has achieved great success as a venture investor, holds the same belief. He wrote, in a special issue of *Newsweek*, that "an unquenchable passion for an idea or a product" is the single "most important ingredient of a company founder. Force venture capitalists to choose between a well-heeled Ivy League student and a smart impoverished immigrant, and we'll pick the latter every time. . . . *Tenacity is a necessity*" [emphasis is mine].

Your Passion Is an Important Part of Determination

One of the seminal management books of the last few years is *Good to Great: Why Some Companies Make the Leap . . . and Others Don't*. In it, Jim Collins and a large team of researchers set out to determine why some companies "make the leap" from a good company to a lasting, great company. Although the book's focus is on Fortune 500 firms, its central findings also have important implications for you.

Collins stresses that successful companies ignite the passions of those involved. He finds that to achieve lasting success, even large companies need people to be excited and energetic about what they are doing. He further notes the special nature of passion: "You can't manufacture passion or 'motivate' people to feel passionate. You can only discover what ignites your passion and the passion of those around you . . . The good-to-great companies did not say, 'Okay, folks, let's get passionate about what we do.' Sensibly they went the other way entirely: We should only do those things that we can get passionate about."

In essence, you must choose a business that ignites your own passion. To prosper, you must combine two factors: your skills and a commitment that releases the excitement and energy that causes you to do your best work and to stick with the enterprise. As you build your business, you will inevitably need a healthy determination and a strong passion to work through the unavoidable ups and downs on the road to success.

In his discussion of passion, Collins makes an additional point: It can be the outcome of your business, not the work itself, that ignites your excitement. "This doesn't mean, however, that you have to be passionate about the mechanics of the business per se (although you might be). The passion circle can be equally focused on what the company stands for. For example, the [Fannie Mae Foundation] people were not passionate about the mechanical process of packaging mortgages into market securities. But they were terrifically motivated by the whole idea of helping people of all classes, backgrounds, and races realize the American dream of owning their home."

ONLY USE OFF-THE-SHELF PRODUCTS AND SERVICES

Over the past few years, the decreasing cost and increasing sophistication of the services available to solo entrepreneurs has expanded dramatically. This expansion and the high value now embedded in off-the-shelf services are central to the successful emergence of go-it-alone businesses.

The discussion here is limited to explaining what is meant by off-the-shelf products and services and why they are central in facilitating the start-up of a go-it-alone business. A far more detailed discussion of these capabilities appears in Chapter 3, "The Great Shift in What's Possible." Today you can subscribe, at almost ridiculously low monthly costs, to a host of services that provide an entire infrastructure for a business. As a result, you can spend almost no capital to get a business off the ground. As noted earlier, you can take advantage of the Yahoo! Store, a full-featured, easy-to-use Internet business hosting and transaction service, for less than $100 per month. The power of these tools cannot be overstated: At least one Silicon Valley start-up scrapped plans for a custom-developed e-commerce Web site, with a budgeted cost in excess of $200,000, after recognizing that the Yahoo! Store could meet its needs.

The implications are significant: Start-up businesses can inexpensively tap sophisticated, state-of-the-art capabilities that were previously available only to larger, wealthier entities. And this is an ongoing process. Lars Hundley, of CleanAirGardening.com, put it this way: "I know that if I see a new capability available for $100,000 on a custom basis, within six months it will be probably be incorporated into the Yahoo! Store as part of the store's basic offering." It also means that entrepreneurs can be assured that most of their critical business functions can be handled through extreme outsourcing, letting them focus their energy and resources on what they do best.

CONCLUSION

In *Thinking for a Change*, John Maxwell discusses the important relationship between what we believe is possible and what we achieve. His insightful notion is that once we hold a specific belief, it changes our expectations, our performance and ultimately what we accomplish: "A belief is not just an idea that you possess; it is an idea that possesses you." Once you believe that it is possible to create a go-it-alone business that lets you do what you do best, you start to act on this idea. Your expectations of what you will accomplish change, and your thinking about how to do things changes. In short, you can start to make it happen. If this is your goal, the following chapters of this book will guide you.

3
THE GREAT SHIFT IN WHAT'S POSSIBLE

The extraordinary transformation, since the early 1990s, in the potential for individuals to influence the business world reflects an unprecedented shift in what is possible. Just a few years ago, most go-it-alone businesses could not have existed or had far more limited potential for profits and growth. We have entered a new era for individual entrepreneurs.

This chapter is divided into four parts. The first part—"More on Central Operating Principles"—explains in greater detail two central operating principles of successful go-it-alone businesses: extreme outsourcing and a relentless focus on enhancement. The second—"The Evolution of the Plug-and-Play Economy"—then discusses the permanent and continuing changes in our economic environment that created the opportunity for these businesses to thrive. The third—"The New Specialization"—addresses the growing role specialization in the economy plays in fostering go-it-alone entities. The final—"Implications of the Hidden Revolution"—describes some of the implications of this new business environment for go-it-alone entrepreneurs.

This chapter has three purposes: First, to provide you with a clear understanding of the underlying principles that make go-it-alone businesses work. Second, to explain the changes occurring in entrepreneurship. Third, to show how go-it-alone businesses can take advantage of new marketplace dynamics.

When you've got the principles down, you can test each business idea and each potential strategy against them. You'll have a mental model of where you're trying to go.

We entrepreneurs are on the cusp of something dramatic. As I discussed the ideas incorporated in this book with multiple businesspeople, one comment has stuck with me: that the businesses I was describing "seem like magic." To me, this comment was both a compliment and a cause for concern. There *is* something special and wonderful about a go-it-alone business—from childhood onward, most of us want to add magic to our lives. But the use of the word magic suggests that successful go-it-alone businesses can't really exist. Nothing could be further from the truth. I have become convinced that we have passed an inflection point: each of the factors that make these businesses both possible and desirable for entrepreneurs is growing stronger with every passing month. This chapter explains why we are just at the beginning of the go-it-alone revolution.

MORE ON CENTRAL OPERATING PRINCIPLES

Extreme Outsourcing

> If I have seen further, it is by standing on the shoulders of giants.
> —*Sir Isaac Newton*

Extreme outsourcing is quite simply doing for your business only what you do best and having someone else do the rest. Today, the "someone else" may not a person at all but a range of inexpensive Internet-based services. These services effectively allow your business to outsource major functions by (1) automating specific activities; (2) providing communications, sales, or marketing capabilities; (3) reducing the effort involved in formerly time-consuming efforts; or (4) managing complex tasks that would otherwise take up large amounts of your time. Sometimes specific activities are outsourced to individuals.

Case Study: Gourmet Outsourcing

Gourmet Gatherings, the unique San Francisco–based culinary entertainment company mentioned earlier, uses extreme outsourcing so that the firm has the capacity to host in excess of 100 events annually without any other full-time employees. This innovative business provides high-end culinary entertainment evenings for corporate and private events. The company contracts with some of the city's finest chefs to lead guests in preparing their own food. Then the attendees are served the gourmet meal they have cooked themselves. The company is growing rapidly and is profitable.

Shannan Bishop, one partner, states that since their business's inception, the two owners have come to view themselves as "conducting a symphony of specialists." Today, Bishop and Bibby Gignilliat, the other founding partner, focus on their innovative menu, marketing, and ways of growing the business. Although they oversee the business itself, they have systematized the activities involved in events to the point that they don't need to attend each event.

Gourmet Gatherings uses a sophisticated mix of technology and part-time contractors (who handle specialized tasks) to run their business: Inbound sales information calls (which are generated through the Web site and word of mouth) are handled by a trained off-site contractor; a separate off-site contractor handles scheduling; and yet another trained contractor responds to e-mail inquiries. In many cases, these contractors are themselves running go-it-alone businesses that specialize in providing these services to multiple companies.

Shannan Bishop has created detailed manuals for how the people staffing Gourmet Gatherings events, from fine chefs to event managers to servers, should handle all aspects of the job. By systematizing each function, Bishop has made it possible to hire part-time employees who want to supplement their day-time earnings by working at night, to grow the business, and to leverage the partners' time by eliminating the need for either of them to attend and oversee events.

The Importance of Focus

In today's extraordinarily competitive economy, you need the freedom to concentrate on making the unique aspects of your business as terrific as possible. And you need the freedom to focus daily on further enhancing your business. With extreme outsourcing, the go-it-alone entrepreneur can, for the first time, do these things.

A number of excellent books have addressed the central importance of focus in achieving business success. A few of the insights provided in this material are shared below. But this book goes a step further to show you how to set up your business to take advantage of the power of focus. In the past, solo entrepreneurs might have recognized the need for focus but as one-man bands found it impossible to establish an infrastructure that really allowed them to develop this capacity. As detailed later in this chapter, new sophisticated capabilities have dramatically changed, in recent years, the ease with which solo entrepreneurs can outsource critical business functions.

An excellent book that describes the strength that anyone can achieve through sustained attention to a problem is *The Power of Focus*. Two of the coauthors, Jack Canfield and Mark Hansen, are also the creators of the *Chicken Soup for the Soul* series. In the introduction, the authors note: "Remember, it's all about focus. *The main reason most people struggle professionally and personally is lack of focus.*" [Emphasis is mine.]

Later, they elaborate on this idea, "Focus on those ideas you do brilliantly, and from which you produce extraordinary results. If you don't you'll probably create high stress levels and ultimate burnout."

But what is focus? In *A Bias for Action: How Effective Managers Harness Their Willpower, Achieve Results, and Stop Wasting Time*, Heike Bruch and Sumantra Ghoshal provide an excellent three-part explanation to the most important aspects of achieving focus in business. They write:

- "First, rather than merely reacting to developments as they arise, or meeting routine requirements, focused managers are goal oriented. They have clear ideas about what they are striving for."
- "Second, focus requires that a manager is intentional, channeling all activities toward achiving the desired goal. That means taking the time to reflect regularly on your own behavior, and being willing and able to choose what you do and do not do each day. Focused behavior does not emerge by chance, nor from the moment."
- "Third, focus requires personal discipline. That means protecting yourself against the usual noise of everyday demands—or exciting opportunities—that will inevitably tug at your attention and emotions. It also means not allowing resistance to keep you from pursuing your goal."

Al Ries's book *Focus: The Future of Your Company Depends on It*, specifically addresses the power that focus can bring to a company. Ries's introduction opens with a compelling analogy:

The sun is a powerful source of energy. Every hour the sun washes the earth with billions of kilowatts of energy. Yet, with a hat and some sunscreen you can bathe in the light of the sun for hours at a time with few ill effects.

A laser is a weak source of energy. A laser takes a few watts of energy and focuses them in a coherent stream of light. But with a laser you can drill a hole in a diamond or wipe out a cancer.

When you focus a company, you create the same effect. You create a powerful, laserlike ability to dominate a market. That's what focusing is all about.

It is this laserlike power that individuals can now achieve by combining extreme outsourcing with personal leverage.

This may sound simple, but in practice it's not. Although the creation of a central objective sounds easy, over time the sometimes mundane work of pushing forward may seem less engaging. It's naturally more exciting to start thinking about new big objectives than to continue working at "singles and doubles," the small wins and big wins that slowly but surely advance the company toward its goal. As detailed in Chapter 3, there is also an inherent, inevitably damaging tendency toward drift. Both small and large companies start out with clear objectives but frequently become distracted by new possibilities that emerge over time.

Failure Is the Inevitable Consequence of a Lack of Focus

John Osher, the successful serial entrepreneur, discussed the flip side of this argument: What happens when focus is lost? In an interview in *Entrepreneur* magazine, Osher cites a lack of focus as one of the most common mistakes that causes start-ups to fail: "Many entrepreneurs go in too many directions at once and do not execute anything well. Rather than focusing on doing everything right to sell to their biggest markets, they divide the attention of their people and their time, trying to do too many things at [one time]."

Similarly, in *Less Is More: How Great Companies Use Produc-*

tivity as the Ultimate Competitive Edge, bestselling author Jason Jennings concludes that the ability to focus on a consistent strategic goal, what Jennings calls a simple "big objective," is the single most significant differentiator between productive and nonproductive companies: "To focus means to concentrate attention or effort. Unfortunately, most corporate leaders act as though they suffer from attention deficit disorder when it comes to keeping their companies focused on mastering a simple BIG objective." Jennings also stresses that focus is not something that shifts from day to day—it is a dedicated concentration on the central skill that allows your company to create value.

And in his memoir, *Who Says Elephants Can't Dance?: Inside IBM's Historic Turnaround*, Lou Gerstner, who engineered IBM's successful turnaround, agrees. Gerstner notes that "few people and institutions would admit to a lack of focus, even in an exercise of honest self-evaluation. However, I have learned that lack of focus is the most common cause of corporate mediocrity."

Set Up the Business So That You Have the Time and Energy to Focus

As noted earlier, it's not uncommon to meet entrepreneurs who will say that they know exactly how to make their businesses thrive—they just need a work week of several hundred hours. By outsourcing as much as possible, you create the equivalent of your own 300-hour work week: You have the time necessary to devote to the specific skills or service that are the basis of your business and its success.

Burnout Is Not a Necessity: It Is a Symptom of a Problem

Developing a successful business means that you will need to work hard and have a high degree of determination. It does not, however, mean that you must be a victim of the burnout that seems so common among entrepreneurs. If you are working hard and not realizing your objectives, you either are trying to do too much or haven't established the appropriate systems to leverage your core skills. In either case, the answer is not to keep slogging on; it is to rethink your systems.

Indeed, success requires ongoing focus and innovation. These vital creative activities cannot be sustained if you suffer from burnout. As a consequence, it is imperative that any signs of imminent burnout be viewed as a symptom of a problem that requires you to change the way you have structured your business.

Hard work is unquestionably a virtue, and a necessity in any start-up. Nonetheless, there is a tendency in American business culture to admire those who work too hard. In a go-it-alone business, it's critical that you not fall into this trap. When you are on your own, there is no boss who watches whether you are working 10 hours a week or 100. It's essential to measure progress by what you have accomplished, not by how hard you have worked at it. Moreover, for you and your business to prosper, you must establish a *sustainable routine* in which you can do your best work and flourish over the long-term.

Consider Your Personal Energy Level

Jim Loehr and Tony Schwartz, the authors of *The Power of Full Engagement: Managing Energy, Not Time, Is the Key to High Performance and Personal Renewal*, make a point that is particularly important in this discussion: It is not simply creating time for focus that is critical—it is also the ability to manage your energy. In establishing your business system, keep in mind that you don't realize any objective if you create time for yourself but don't set up the system so that you also have the energy to use that time well. The value of extreme outsourcing is that it frees you from handling the vast majority of activities that eat away at both your energy and your time.

Creating Time and Energy for Constant Reinvention

Though it has become almost a cliché to say that you need to constantly reinvent your business, that need is a stark reality. In the few short years that Speed Anywhere has existed, I've needed to completely reinvent the source of the business's strength four times. Each of these reinventions has involved the development of a completely new means of marketing the service in response to changes in the market or in efforts by the competition. In each case, the business would have suffered a near total death had I not reinvented its core marketing propositions. As a go-it-alone entrepreneur, I had the time to maintain the competitive vitality of the business only because of extreme outsourcing. From its inception, I assumed that the business would require constant reinvention, and I built this into my operating schedule.

What this means is that you can never rest on your laurels. You must be constantly moving forward. The time you need for this constant innovation can be found through outsourcing absolutely everything possible. Reinvention cannot be placed on the to-do list of long-term problems that you'll address after you do everything else. Business conditions and your competitive standing can shift in a matter of weeks. You want to have the time and energy *daily* to focus on how your business will look next week and next month. You can do this only if you outsource everything that is not part of your core source of business strength.

The Outsourcing Advantage: Inexpensively Keeping You at the Cutting Edge

Subsequent sections of this chapter discuss the constant evolution and reinvention of outsourcing providers. These services must be at the cutting edge of sophistication to attract and keep clients, a further benefit to you because these providers must offer state-of-the-art solutions to keep their customers satisfied. As a consequence, for a small monthly subscription fee, your business is always able to access the same cutting-edge solutions that were previously available only to the largest companies.

Outsourcing Doesn't Mean a Function Is Nonessential

You may believe that if a business owner lets someone else handle a function or service, it can't be as important as things done in-house. But that's a misconception. The goal for any go-it-alone business is to provide a distinctive service or product that meets the needs of its customers. This doesn't mean that every critical function—or every aspect of a critical function—has to be handled in-house. You are providing the customer with the result of your total business system.

Firms in many industries outsource important functions precisely because they want the benefits of an entity that specializes in a critical area. In the drug industry, clinical trials are an essential component of drug development, yet the industry is increasingly outsourcing this function. A unit of Pharmaceutical Product Development, Inc., for example, specializes in clinical trials for drug manufacturers and has worked with nearly all of the world's largest 50 companies. Things are similar in the oil industry.

As one authoritative article on outsourcing notes: "Schlumberger offers such superior competency in drilling that oil companies have little choice but to outsource. Why spend more to do it yourself when you can spend less and get it done better?"

To determine whether outsourcing is appropriate for you, ask yourself this: *Even if a function is critical to my business, can it be handled as well or better and cost-effectively by an available service?* If the answer is yes, then you should outsource it. You will be competitively hurt if you don't take advantage of available low-cost services. Your competitors inevitably will use these or similar services and will then have the time to focus their energies on their unique service.

Case Study: KaBoom Beverages

Wyck Hay's first entrepreneurial initiative was an unqualified success: He was the cofounder of herbal tea maker Celestial Seasonings, and he helped sell the company to Kraft Foods for $40 million in 1984. His experience, substantial resources, and track record suggest that it's worth taking note of how he chose to set up his new business venture.

In 2002, Hay launched KaBoom Beverages Inc. (www .KaBoomBev.com), which produces a high-energy juice drink for health-conscious consumers. A friend offered Hay a taste of Red Bull, an imported energy-boosting drink. Hay says, " I woke up the next morning, and said, 'I can make the product ten times better at a reduced cost and with added value for consumers who don't like carbonation, fructose, refined sugars, and high levels of caffeine and artificial this and that.'"

Hay determined that the most effective way to build the business was to outsource absolutely everything. He assembled outside contractors to handle all of the operational aspects—from manufacturing to label design—of a business that will exceed $2 million. Hay is the firm's sole employee.

He believes that extreme outsourcing has benefited Kaboom in multiple ways. Hay estimates that his expenses are at least 30% below what he would be paying for the same activities in-house. The reasons behind why such savings are discussed at length later in this chapter (see "The Evolution of the Plug-and-Play Economy," pages 58–69). It's worth noting, however, that they reflect the economics of *outsourcing,* not *offshoring.* "All of my providers do their work in this country [the United States]," Hay says.

Hay also benefits by working with entities that have high

expertise in their particular activities. Choosing the right providers for each function is essential. "I spent at least as much time in choosing providers for outsourcing as we used to spend in the interview process for hiring employees at Celestial Seasonings," he says.

Hay is emphatic in his bias toward action, his approach to ongoing experimentation, and his belief in learning directly from customers. In the summers of 2002 and 2003, he and his wife set up free sampling tables outside retail stores and asked each consumer for comments. "At the end of each day, we would compile the results and modify the product flavors for our next production run based on what we learned," he said. Customer feedback also helped Hay to determine the most attractive names for the three flavors of his drinks. Hay estimates that through this process he had direct contact with an astounding number of people: "We have probably spoken face-to-face with 20,000 to 30,000 people who sampled our product," he says.

Of perhaps greatest importance, extreme outsourcing allows Hay to focus his time and energy on creating a product with the highest possible customer appeal, which he believes is the key to the success of the business. Although Hay participated in managing 300 employees at Celestial Seasonings, "I didn't want a lot of employees at KaBoom Beverages. I knew that employee maintenance was very time-consuming for somebody who wanted to be creative in the development of the product line," he says.

A Constant Focus on Experimentation and Enhancement

Relentless repeatability allows entrepreneurs to create a leveraged business. Extreme outsourcing provides the time and energy to focus on the core attributes of the business. The final piece of this puzzle is the use of time: Successful entrepreneurs are focused on constantly improving their product or service, and they exhibit four distinct attributes:

Go-it-alone entrepreneurs understand the cumulative value of singles and doubles. The mythology of innovation tends to focus on a single grand slam that dramatically invents or reinvents a business. The reality is that success is more typically the result of cumulative, almost prosaic hard work, where the entrepreneur is constantly asking himself or herself, "Now how can I make this better?" or "What can I do to reduce these costs, even if it's only by a small amount?" Over time, this dedication to ongoing improvement builds up: The cumulative effect of many singles and doubles is often a home run—a total business system.

In *Profitable Growth Is Everyone's Business*, Ram Charan elaborates on this idea: "In baseball, the home run, especially in crucial, big-game situations, is electrifying and exciting. In business, the big, bold idea, the breakthrough disruptive technology, the new product that will revolutionize the marketplace . . . are similarly exhilarating. But there is a problem: Home runs don't happen every day or even every decade." The business that relies on home runs for ongoing success is, as Charan notes, likely to be waiting a very long time. By focusing on dramatic change, these businesses are also far more likely to miss the opportunity to systematically exploit smaller opportunities and to fail to adapt to constant changes in the marketplace.

Charan instead advocates the process followed by successful go-it-alone entrepreneurs:

A surer and more consistent path—one that does not exclude home runs—is what I call going for "singles and doubles," growth based on improvements or natural extensions of the strategy, business model, customer needs, or technology of a business. These singles and doubles can come from adapting to major changes in the marketplace as well as relatively small day-to-day wins. . . .

Singles and doubles do not come from looking in the rearview mirror. . . . Rather, they are a result of looking at the business from the outside-in, from customer needs backward into the company. The impact of singles and doubles can be huge. In fact they form the foundation for the home run.

Here is one example of this type of thinking:

- Laura Walker, president and CEO of WNYC Radio (www .WNYC.org), the National Public Radio affiliate in the New York metropolitan area, is an entrepreneur at a nonprofit. She led the group that shifted the station's status from ownership by New York City to independent nonprofit. Under her leadership, the station, in 7 years, increased its revenues from $8 million to $23 million, increased the size of its listening base from 650,000 to 1.1 million, and became the number-one radio station (as measured by audience size) in Manhattan. This is particularly impressive because during the same period, the total number of commercial radio listeners in New York City declined.

  Walker explains her approach by noting that there is "no single magic bullet. You add to the quality of the service and your membership recruitment piece by piece, brick by brick." She also notes that the growing strength of a foundation built on singles and doubles is particularly important because, "each thing we build takes us one step forward and allows us to build to the next level. You can only build a terrific service over time with lots of attention to the small wins that slowly but inexorably move you forward."

Go-it-alone business owners orient their product development around what they learn from customers. Because these companies have always lived off positive cash flow from customers—as opposed to investor dollars—they are particularly sensitive to finding ever better ways to meet customer needs.

Go-it-alone entrepreneurs translate their experimental attitude into actual experiments. In the areas that are part of their core focus, they are constantly asking themselves, "What if . . . ?" As one such entrepreneur says, "You test and you test, and then you test some more." This idea may seem self-evident, but it's incredibly easy to overlook this process, particularly in a one-person operation. That's why as the business expands, outsourcing everything you can and being disciplined are essential.

Maintaining an experimental attitude also means that go-it-alone entrepreneurs are oriented toward *doing* something as opposed to *thinking about doing* something. Go-it-alone entrepreneurs are not obsessed with attempting to know everything possible about a subject before they act on it. In contrast, they believe that no matter how much they study a possible action they won't really know what matters until they get started. They believe that you learn by doing and by live experimentation.

As a consequence, go-it-alone entrepreneurs are impatient. They know that they are unlikely to "get it right" the first time, so they limit the risk associated with whatever they are doing. They begin with small steps. At the same time, they also know that the only way to ultimately "get it right" is to get started as quickly as possible.

Go-it-alone entrepreneurs recognize that mistakes are a necessary part of the game. As a solo entrepreneur, your attitude toward mistakes is, in fact, so important for your ultimate success, that it is the focus of Chapter 13 of this book, "Mistakes Happen—Learn from Them."

THE EVOLUTION OF THE PLUG-AND-PLAY ECONOMY

The Rule of Decreasing Support Costs

In *The Tipping Point: How Little Things Make a Big Difference*, Malcolm Gladwell effectively describes how a series of small changes ultimately lead to a cascading effect, in which a quantum shift occurs. Such a shift is exactly what has happened since the late-1990s with regard to the availability of easy-to-use services over the Internet and the resulting increase in possibilities for go-it-alone entrepreneurs.

Today, almost everyone is familiar with Moore's law, which holds that every 18 months computing power doubles while the price drops by one half. My decade of experience in the Internet technology arena has led me to postulate a similar rule for the capabilities available to businesses—the Rule of Decreasing Support Costs: Services that are available today at high expense for large businesses will be available in 12 to 18 months on a plug-and-play outsourced basis to small companies at low monthly usage fees. The examples of this kind of rapid evolution are endless: A few years ago, the cost of systems designed to host and process payments for Internet retailers could exceed one hundred thousand dollars a year. Today, a system with equal or better functionality is available for $14.95 a month. At one time, large information technology firms offered to build intranets for Fortune 500 businesses at a cost of millions of dollars. Today, these same services are accessible, on an outsourced basis, to a small firm at less than $100 a month.

What matters for this discussion is not the Rule of Decreasing Costs in itself but its dramatic implications. The drastic drop in the cost of sophisticated services has made it possible for a solo enterprise to use and automate the same productivity-enhancing services that have made larger companies successful, and to automate this entire effort. This capability is now so robust that it represents a quantum change in what was once available and in how entrepreneurs can go about starting new businesses. In part, this change levels the playing field between large companies and smaller ones. Amazingly, the business community has generally overlooked this huge change, effectively dismissing the idea of successful go-it-alone enterprises.

The Rise of the Application Service Provider (ASP)

The acronym *ASP* stands for *application service provider*. It's important that you not be intimidated by this technical term. ASPs are essentially software transformed into easy-to-use on-demand services. For our purposes, an ASP can be simply defined as

A service of any kind (ranging from QuickBooks online to sales-force management systems such as Salesforce.com to automated credit-card authorization services to payroll management from companies such as ADP, to 401(k) management from companies such as Fidelity) that is available instantly via the Internet, where the user does not install or operate the underlying software and typically pays for the service on a subscription basis.

Several factors make ASPs significant. First, they are designed to be easy to use. Most ASPs are created for mainstream businesspeople who have neither the time nor the inclination to learn how to use difficult programs. Indeed, at the dawn of the Internet era, I wrote an award-winning newsletter that selected the best ASPs available for small businesses. I had one firm criterion for deciding on recommendations: Any ASP that took more than 10 minutes to learn was immediately disqualified!

Rick Mosenkis, the CEO and cofounder of Trichys, which operates WorkZone (www.MyWorkZone.com), explains how his company has embraced this defining criteria. "With WorkZone, our customers can establish extranets [shared secure "filing cabinets" on the Web that allow for collaboration] for their clients within 45 seconds. The most important feature of this ASP service is that it is easy for everyone to use." He adds that "Customers want an intuitive way to solve their problems. Today, when you make a phone call you don't think of all the technology involved. Our focus is for users to have a similar experience with WorkZone. So, our service must be simple to use and our powerful technology must be invisible."

Second, ASPs are a shared-cost model. The service is developed once, then can be shared by thousands of users, so the costs are inherently low. To the user, the cost savings from relying on an ASP are similar to those from traveling as one of many airline passengers instead of chartering a private jet for personal use. There is an additional, growing benefit here: the extraordinary ability for users to now customize most ASPs to meet their specific needs, which is discussed later in this chapter. To turn the earlier analogy on its head, customization allows the user to fly his or her own private jet—at a coach fare.

Third, the software for ASPs is run at a central location, typically the home office. As a consequence, ASP developers can continuously upgrade the product. Each upgrade is instantly available to every user who logs onto the service via the Internet. Moreover, in response to competitive pressures, most ASPs take advantage of this low-upgrade distribution cost, allowing them to be continuously improved. It's not unusual to subscribe to an ASP at one price and then discover, a few months later, that for the same price the value of the service, as measured by its features, has literally doubled!

Several aspects of ASPs that are particularly relevant to the go-it-alone entrepreneur. First, thousands of inexpensive ASPs are now available for almost every imaginable business activity: human resources management, sales management, financial management, customer service, e-mail, sales, marketing, purchasing, collaboration, and much more. In essence, there is almost no service that cannot be outsourced via the ASP model today. This explosion in ASPs has made them the backbone of the go-it-alone business. A successful entrepreneur decides on the type of business to enter, and then leverages his or her skills through extreme outsourcing to multiple ASPs. (See "Resources for Getting Started" on page 206 for a list of particularly valuable ASPs. A more comprehensive, up-to-date list of recommended ASPs for go-it-alone entrepreneurs can be found at www.BruceJudson.com).

Second, the ongoing development of ASPs is one unstoppable trend that levels the playing field between big companies and firms run by individuals. Small businesses can now compete with big businesses.

Third, even more sophisticated time-saving ASPs are on the horizon. At the start of this section, I noted that success is all about time and limiting energy-draining distractions. One of the principal benefits of ASPs is their ability to manage complex tasks and free the solo entrepreneur to focus on what matters most.

In an interview with CRMIQ (www.crmiq.com) for its online site, Michael Doyle, chairman and CEO of Salesnet (www.Salesnet.com), an online provider of sales tracking and customer-relationship management (CRM) services, cited multiple benefits of ASP use by smaller firms:

- **Faster return on investment:** Because the online model can be "deployed in days or weeks—not months or years," with minimal training time, customers see a fast return on their spending.

- **No required infrastructure:** With online services, no hardware or software is needed. "You just point your browser."
- **Unbeatable affordability:** "There are no setup fees, maintenance payments or other hidden costs—just one simple monthly subscription that is less than your sales rep's cell phone bill. . . . And because online companies can spread the cost of their infrastructure across tens-of-thousands of users, staying ahead of the technology curve is never a burdensome cost to the customer, or a needless distraction to a successful business."
- **Unlimited scalability:** Online CRM solutions are less complex and provide feature-rich functionality that is fully configurable by customers. Application enhancements are seamless and instantaneous. Because these solutions are fully scalable, they can easily meet the demands of growing enterprises.

Because many go-it-alone businesses rely on a large number of independently operating ASPs, the current focus of many ASPs is on easy integration with other ASPs. As businesses link functions, much less time is required to ensure that information residing in one "silo" is incorporated into other aspects of the business. The same holds true for integrating information in ASPs with commonly used software. Salesnet, for example, offers more than 200 prebuilt connectors to software such as Lotus Notes and Oracle. Doyle says that like Salesnet itself, they are easy to use: "They are configured by clicks, not code. This represents an accelerating trend. Over time, there will soon be ever more easy to use, sophisticated links between ASPs and commonly used software and between ASPs communicating with other ASPs. The result will be an increasingly seamless experience for the small-business user.

Essential for go-it-alone entrepreneurs is the accelerated development of ASPs targeted at businesses with fewer employees. The list of ASP resources at the back of this book is a small fraction of what's available, while the larger array of ASPs listed at the Web site for this book (www.BruceJudson.com) still don't capture the full magnitude of what's available. Each day seems to bring multiple announcements of new services or sophisticated improvements to existing services that will help boost the productivity of go-it-alone businesses. This suggests that we haven't seen anything yet.

Amazon.com, eBay, Google, & Yahoo!

In closing this discussion of ASPs, it's worth noting that the four companies that are arguably the most successful Internet businesses all operate a range of ASP services designed to support go-it-alone entrepreneurs. In many cases, the ASP services operated by Amazon.com, eBay, Google, and Yahoo! provide the basic infrastructure that makes it possible for many go-it-alone businesses to exist.

A portion of the activities of these companies include:

- **eBay auction services,** which support hundreds of thousands of entrepreneurs.
- **Google AdWords,** which provides highly targeted pay-per-click advertising, and allows even the smallest businesses to reach a nationwide or worldwide audience within a few minutes of enrolling.
- **Google AdSense,** which allows entrepreneurs to easily generate advertising revenues from their online content.
- **Yahoo! Merchant Solutions,** which provides sophisticated e-commerce services to start-up businesses.
- **Overture Precision Match** (owned by Yahoo!), which also provides easy-to-use targeted pay-per-click advertising to start-up firms.

- **Amazon.com's Associates program** (the first online affiliate program of its kind with over 900,000 members), which allows entrepreneurs to create their own specialty stores with Amazon.com providing the products, as well as the necessary commerce and fulfillment services.

The extensive involvement of these four firms in fostering go-it-alone ventures is more than a coincidence. It's a strong indication of the growing demand for go-it-alone services: These companies generate substantial revenues by providing ever more innovative services to start-up entrepreneurs. It's also a strong demonstration of the growing vitality of go-it-alone businesses. In cases such as Google's AdSense program and Amazon.com's Associates program, these large firms significantly enhance their own profits by making it simple for entrepreneurs to create specialized businesses using their services, with the entrepreneur and the larger firm sharing the resulting revenues.

Case Study: How Application Service Providers Create a Business Opportunity for China Manufacturing Network

Everette Phillips is cofounder of China Manufacturing Network, LLC (www.sourceglobally.com/CMN/), in Irvine, California. The company has established relationships with nearly 100 family-owned factories in China. In the United States, the company has built a substantial customer base of small companies that are seeking to have parts manufactured in China quickly and cost-effectively. In the past, this kind of offshore matchmaking service would have involved high complexity (in processing, negotiating, and tracking each order) and required significant numbers of employees. But Phillips was able to create a go-it-alone business that relies on an ASP to handle a complex supply chain. China Manufacturing Network's precision-manufacturing division takes the orders for manufactured parts from small U.S. companies online. Then, it handles price negotiation, creation and approval of prototypes, production arrangements, sales tracking, inventory management, and online invoicing. "We are like a general contractor," says Phillips. "When a purchase order comes in, we assume the responsibility for getting the product made and shipped."

Phillips's business, which also sends blueprints of parts to Chinese factories, runs without an information technology (IT) department. Phillips relies entirely on the sophisticated capabilities of NetSuite, an ASP for CRM and enterprise resource planning (ERP). That leaves him free to work on building the business, to work with customers, to develop services with competitive prices, and to manage independent sales reps. The mechanics of the business are already taken care of. Phillips estimates that without NetSuite or a similar ASP, his company would need an IT staff of 5 to 10 people just to handle its current workload. He credits the use of NetSuite with keeping his company at the cutting edge of capabilities—the ASP is constantly upgrading the quality of its offerings.

Before forming China Manufacturing with a partner, Phillips, age 44, had had a lengthy career in the United States and Europe with Seiko Instruments. While there, he held several positions, including general manager for advanced manufacturing technology. Why did such an experienced corporate executive choose to start a go-it-alone venture? "We originally had a plan for a larger, more all-encompassing business, but when we saw how much we would need to give away in raising venture funding, it became less interesting," he says. So the two partners took the piece of the business that they could build on their own and used their own funds for start-up. In essence they followed the 80/20 rule: They focused on the high-leverage piece of their business idea, which could generate the most value with the least investment. This allowed them to get the business off the ground and to retain ownership, so that they will realize the full rewards of whatever they create.

Application Service Providers and the Rise of Mass Customization

A central aspect of the continuing evolution of outsourcing is mass customization, the ability of ASPs, as well as brick-and-mortar, to provide such a variety of features and options that different users can effectively customize an existing service to meet their precise needs. The WorkZone APS, for example, is designed so that service firms, such as ad agencies, can create extranets with distinct features for each client. Rick Mosenkis, CEO of Trichys, which owns WorkZone says, "One ad agency might be operating different extranets with very different functions for 15 different clients, all based on preset options in our easy-to-use service."

Outsourced services of all kinds generally follow the same pattern of growth and development. First, the service is launched with a minimum level of potential customization. The service performs a valuable function well, but it's one size fits all.

The next phase of the life cycle is central to supporting go-it-alone businesses. As the ASP matures, it typically ads robust features that allow clients to create an increasingly customized experience. For example, when I first started Speed Anywhere, I was delighted to find a low-cost provider that (1) allowed me to inexpensively create a customized form that users would fill out on my Web site, (2) stored the information in a database, and (3) simultaneously e-mailed the information to as many different people as I specified. Eighteen months later, there were services available that performed all of those functions *and* had several far more sophisticated attributes. Now, for approximately the same cost, I can link the information collected to a database and in real time display information back to the consumer. I can also customize the routing of the e-mails so that different individuals and companies receive leads based on the information provided by the customer. When the business was first established, this was one of the few functions that I retained in-house, because I could not locate a service that would be more cost effective—for the volume involved—than quickly sorting these leads on a daily basis. These advances allow me to tailor the multiple functions of the application in a way that is best for my business, yet other users of the same service can tailor these same functions in a completely different way for their businesses.

This kind of advance reflects the Rule of Decreasing Support Costs discussed earlier. It's my guess that in 2002, it would have cost me a minimum of $50,000 in programming for even a rudimentary function that could query a database, provide real-time feedback to consumers within an easy-to-understand interface, and intelligently route the information provided to different people. This is precisely the service I described above, and in 2004, it's available for less than $30.00 per month.

This aspect of ASP development—customizability for users—is in its infancy. The ASP industry has started to focus on customization as a key area of competition—with multiple reports in the trade press as companies work to outdo one another at customization. This means that we can anticipate a quantum jump in the degree to which individual firms of any size can customize basic services.

Case Study: Sophisticated E-mail Management Services

Here's part of an e-mail distributed by JangoMail, the ASP discussed earlier. The company hosts customer e-mail lists and allows for easy management of targeted mailings. JangoMail informed me that it had added a new customization feature:

Today we are pleased to announce a new feature which allows for greater personalization within the body of your e-mail messages. Dynamic messaging and conditional logic allow you to compose and send one e-mail, but have different content display to different recipients based on their demographic profile.

For example, if you are the e-marketing coordinator for an Internet sporting goods store called SportsDeals.com, you may want to send out an e-mail of special deals to all of your past customers. You may want your customers who play tennis to receive a promotion about tennis equipment and you may want your skiing customers to receive a promotion about skiing equipment. And you may want everyone else to receive a generic promotion on any product within the store.

You can accomplish this by inserting simple IF-THEN-ELSE statements within the body of your e-mail. . . .

This example is included not to recommend the JangoMail service but to demonstrate the unending, almost daily march of customization. ASPs like JangoMail are constantly working to build additional features that create ever more power for users. It's not that any one service or innovation makes a huge difference. It's that the *sum* of each of these innovations adds (the singles and doubles) a new level of power to the entrepreneur's capabilities. These singles and doubles accumulate, making the go-it-alone business far stronger with each passing month.

We can look at the JangoMail advancement from multiple perspectives. First, it follows the Rule of Decreasing Support Costs. A new level of powerful customization is now available at a lower cost than previously because JangoMail has increased the power of its service without raising price.

Second, a JangoMail user could previously have accomplished the same end results offered by the new customization, but only through extending far more time and energy—the most precious commodities available to go-it-alone entrepreneurs. By making powerful services easily accessible, ASPs help entrepreneurs expand their businesses on a level playing field shared by larger companies.

Third, according to Ajay Goel, the company's CEO, JangoMail has developed a clear system for continuously improving its service and ensuring that customers recognize this ongoing innovation. "We try to have a significant feature enhancement that we can announce each month. We want our customers to see that we are continuously adding value to the service at no extra cost." JangoMail's development efforts follow clear, customer-focused goals. Goel says, "Our first priority is to add the features customers tell us they want. Next, we look to add the features that we see our competitors are offering that we don't have yet. The last item on the list are the features that we think are valuable."

There is a fourth phenomenon, one not yet discussed in this book: In many cases, the addition of new features to an application will spark ideas for new business initiatives on the part of ASP subscribers. I have experienced this myself. An ASP that supports my business will announce a new feature, and I will start to think, *I can increase my business by using this feature to* . . . So another value of using ASPs is that they can kick-start your plans for improving your own business. It's a lot of work to develop a new marketing idea from scratch. It's far easier when you are looking at an easy-to-use capability that is already part of your business and think, *Now I can use this to* ____ *at no additional cost, and my total time investment will be* ____.

THE NEW SPECIALIZATION

What I am about to write probably classifies me as extremist or, at minimum, effusive. But I'll say it anyway: I believe that we have entered the beginning of a new era of specialization that, for better or worse, may rival Henry Ford's creation of the automobile.

Specialization in Retailing

We are witnessing the rise of specialization in several distinct ways. The first area, highly targeted retailing, seems relatively obvious. It is now far easier for anyone who wants to make a living offering a specialized service or product to find sufficient customers to make this possible. CleanAirGardening.com is one example. A store dedicated to ecologically oriented gardening supplies probably could not draw enough traffic in the physical world to survive—there might not be sufficient interest in any particular local community. However, in the online world, the store's potential community expands to at least the entire United States. Within this far larger community, there are enough people with an interest in ecologically oriented gardening supplies to support at least one dedicated store. Search engines make it possible for such people to learn about the store. Similarly, the majority of eBay stores cater to a very specific interest. The owners of these stores make money because eBay helps them aggregate customers.

Unbundling and Specialization in Corporate Organization

The second aspect of specialization, which most likely has more far-reaching consequences, is that global networking inherently leads to the unbundling of just about everything. Two business that are examples of such unbundling have already been discussed: Mr. Trademark, which unbundled the trademark search process from the lawyer's job of interpreting the results of the search, and Speed Anywhere, which unbundled the broadband sales process into three separate tasks of (1) finding potential broadband prospects, (2) selling specific services to these prospects, and (3) installing the broadband services. To provide a frame of reference for your analysis of business opportunities, this section briefly explains the theoretical basis for the unbundling of businesses.

In an award-winning 1999 article in the *Harvard Business Review* entitled "Unbundling the Corporation," John Hagel and Marc Singer demonstrated that global electronic networks (that is, the Internet) would cause a dramatic realignment in what was necessarily "inside" and what was "outside" individual firms. Their argument can be abbreviated as follows:

- "Electronic networks allow companies to communicate and exchange data far more quickly and cheaply than ever before. This has created a systematic reduction in interaction costs, which comprise the money and time expended whenever goods, services or ideas are exchanged."
- Interaction costs are the daily tasks of coordination and exchanges within or outside firms. "In a very real sense interaction costs are the friction within the economy. Interaction costs determine how companies organize themselves and their relationships with other parties." If the interaction costs for an activity are lower within a firm, then activities stay under the same roof. If not, they migrate outside the firm.
- An individual company participates in three separate businesses: (1) a customer relations, (2) a product innovation, and (3) an infrastructure (managing repetitive operational tasks).
- The low costs of interaction in an Internet economy will lead firms to specialize in aspects of these three areas and will create new arrangements among different firms specializing in different areas.

In essence, there will be an unbundling followed by new forms of rebundling, with different types of alliances arising to take advantage of these shifting dynamics.

Unbundling Leads to Specialized Businesses

For the go-it-alone business, the third aspect of specialization is particularly important. As the Internet becomes an increasing part of our lives, we can anticipate an increasing emergence of businesses performing highly specialized services. This growth in specialized services, like those provided by Everette Phillips's China Manufacturing Network, will create an increasing array of opportunities for go-it-alone entrepreneurs. As interaction costs go down, activities that were formerly part of one company are unbundled, to be handled by specialized firms that perform an activity and seamlessly integrate it into a web of activities faster or cheaper than when the activity is handled in-house.

Both Mr. Trademark and Speed Anywhere demonstrate this phenomenon. But they're not the only ones.

Case Study: The Investment Management Business

The typical investment management business is composed of several partners and their support staff. The staff members are people with various skill specialties. Increasingly, this traditional model is being supplanted by a model of specialized businesses located across the country that provide customized support to the individual investment adviser.

Eric Goldstone, a highly successful go-it-alone investment adviser, located in Clinton Corners, N.Y., believes that independent investment managers must possess two core skills: "A systematic approach to investing that reflects your underlying methodology, and the ability to educate clients so that they understand your approach and have confidence in it." Where these core skills are not involved, investment advisers can now decide which functions they want to keep in-house and which functions they want to outsource.

- In 1998, David Drucker, one of the nation's top investment advisers, decided, for lifestyle reasons, to move from Washington, D.C. to Albuquerque, New Mexico. Drucker was named to *Worth* magazine's list of the nation's best advisers from 1994 through 2001. In the move, Drucker retained 45 East Coast accounts but did not want to reestablish a traditional office with multiple employees. In Washington, he had had one partner and several employees. Drucker concluded that he could build a virtual office by working with a variety of independent providers, that this setup would allow him to efficiently operate without employees, and that it would lead both to a higher profit margin and a personally more rewarding business.

  Drucker did not want employees largely because of the high responsibility they represent. He believes that if he has employees, he must be responsible not just for their financial well-being but also for mentoring them. When he moved to New Mexico (at about age 50), he was at the stage of his life that he no longer wanted this burden.

- Other successful investment advisers, such as Greg Curry of Louisville, Kentucky, operate without employees for an entirely different reason: They feel they are not talented employers. "Managing employees, for me, is always a train wreck," says Curry in an industry publication. "Doing things this way, I believe I can be a lot more efficient. I've backed into what this business needs to generate so I can have a good life without causing me to have to work eighty hours a week, half of that managing other people," he adds.

- An important aspect of the investment management business is sending accurate, timely reports to clients. These reports must meet certain regulatory requirements, and they require that a skilled individual download and format the information from the client's brokerage or custodial account. Krisan's BackOffice (www.Krisan.com), a go-it-alone firm run by

Krisan Marotta, has developed an expertise in providing this type of complex reporting. Krisan's clients are quick to point out that it would cost them far more to hire and train a full-time reporting person—and to do so repeatedly because of high turnover, which would reduce the all-important time they can put into working with clients.

Krisan's BackOffice has about 20 clients located in 16 U.S. states. Marotta says that working from her home office, she makes "quite a good living. People will pay a lot for a job they know will be done well without supervision." Her flexible work hours mesh well with her other very important job as a mom.

A full analysis of the different functions involved in the unbundling of the investment management business can be found in the book David Drucker wrote with Joel Bruckenstein, *Virtual-Office Tools for a High-Margin Practice*, and their newsletter *Virtual Office News* (www.virtualofficetools.net). It seems likely that this industry is unbundling faster than others because of the very distinct job functions and skills involved in what was formerly a single business. Each person can build a business around his or her particular skill and work as part of a chain, without needing physical proximity to the other members of the chain. Marotta, for example, has worked with clients for over a decade whom she has never met face-to-face. In essence, the decreased interaction costs (to borrow the terminology of Hagel and Singer) brought about by the use of low-cost Internet-based tools and communications make it more effective for these specialists to operate on their own.

Case Study: Spinning for Success

A second example of how specialization and unbundling are changing the shape of business involves one of 2004's hottest new toys, the i-TOP. The i-TOP is an electronic top that, among other things, uses a flashing red light-emitting diode to display the number of spins achieved with a single twist. The top counts these revolutions by comparing its position to the magnetic field of the Earth, and users can compete to see who can achieve the most spins with a single twist. The i-TOP, retailed in the United States for approximately $10.99, and its manufacturer anticipated that the top would sell approximately 3.5 million units in 2004, the first full year of its release. It was projected that of that total, 2 million units would be sold in North America and 1.5 million would be sold in other parts of the globe.

The story of how the i-TOP was brought to market dramatically demonstrates today's growing opportunities for individuals with particular specialties to make things happen—the go-it-alone revolution. Bob Fuhrer, the Manhattan-based president of Nextoy, LLC (www.Nextoy.com) has built a successful business because he makes things happen. He was approached by the top's inventor, who is located in Israel, and agreed to oversee an initiative to bring the top to market. Ordinarily, Fuhrer would have attempted to interest one of the major toy manufacturers, such as Hasbro or Mattel, in licensing the product. However, Fuhrer says two factors influenced him: First, the i-TOP had a unique potential, so he wanted to play a particularly active role in ensuring its success. Second, "there was something new happening in the toy industry." He recognized that the industry had reached the point where he could easily find the best specialists for each aspect of development and bring the toy to market by working with a collection of entities.

Fuhrer identified a manufacturer for the product, Irwin Toy (www.IrwinToy.com) in Canada, and a small, independent design firm located in San Francisco. Irwin Toy, which has only three full-time employees and four contract consultants, is in itself a go-it-alone initiative. Irwin outsourced the packaging and manufacturing of the product and employed an independent sales rep to market the toy to Wal-Mart and other major distributors. Thus, the i-TOP team ultimately involved at least four different go-it-alone businesses, scattered across North America, who provided specialized services. In the past, the majority of these specialized activities would have been located within one company, under the same roof.

The first Irwin Toy was, at one time, Canada's largest toy company. It was sold by the Irwin family, managed badly by the new owners, and ended up in bankruptcy. In 2003, George Irwin and his brother Peter decided to take a shot at reinventing the family business, so they bought back the company name. For this new Toronto-based incarnation, the brothers decided to limit their risk through a very specific approach to the business. First, they concluded, as Bob Fuhrer had, that there was no longer a need to handle everything in-house. "We could get up and running faster and far less expensively by relying on total outsourcing," said George Irwin. Second, they believed that they could limit their risk by focusing on variations of toys with proven appeal. They were enthusiastic about the i-TOP because, as George Irwin notes, "This is an exciting modern variation on a product with proven appeal. Tops have been around for a long time."

George Irwin recognizes that his company is at the forefront of a new, more profitable business model. He says that he and his brother managed to start "a large toy business without raising a great deal of money." Although they did borrow some funds through mortgages on their homes, it was a small amount compared with the capital once needed to become a serious entrant in the toy business. He says,

We absolutely could not have created the i-TOP in the same way five years ago. The easy ability to communicate through the Internet made all the difference. In the past, if you worked with people in other locations, you had to physically send them pictures. Each change required another set of pictures and introduced delays into the process. Now, we can be looking at a prospective rendering via the Internet, the designer can be located anywhere, and we can agree upon and instantly see changes to the design in real time. You can't underestimate the importance of this kind of collaborative tool, particularly since we were rushing to meet a delivery deadline. We are working with specialists we have never met face-to-face. It's just impossible to imagine this kind of thing happening just a few years ago.

Irwin believes that in certain situations, small firms relying on outsourced teams have an advantage over their larger competitors. "Typically, it takes eight to ten months to bring a product to market. The demand for the i-TOP was so high that we did it in four months. This, in itself, is a remarkable accomplishment."

Case Study: Marketing in the Health Insurance Business

A final example of unbundling and rebundling resulting from the growth of the Internet is the rise of financial services—including health insurance—sold through Internet-based comparison services. The largest player in this arena is eHealthInsurance (www.eHealthInsurance.com).

Here's how it works: For individual health insurance companies, a major source of new policies is the aggregator, such as eHealthInsurance, which provides consumers with extraordinary choice among many plans from top health insurance companies in each state. Through its Web site, eHealthInsurance leads prospective customers through more than 4,000 policies from over 140 health insurance companies nationwide to compare available offerings for their geographic location. (You can see this resource at www.HealthPlansToday.com.) This business has bundled an unprecedented number of competitive offerings to create value for consumers and businesses seeking health insurance services. In addition, consumers can complete an online application for the health insurance plan of their choice, pay for it, and sign for it electronically. This service reduces the time it traditionally takes to get health insurance by 4 to 6 weeks, thereby further leveraging the power of the Internet.

The company is not the only one providing comparison bundles, so the Internet marketing battle rages. Under the guidance of Phillip Kidwell, eHealthInsurance has established one of the largest and most successful affiliate marketing programs. Kidwell, the affiliate channel manager, oversees relationships with 2,500 independent marketing entities who all market the eHealth-Insurance comparison service to consumers and receive a fee for each resulting application. However, unlike traditional insurance agents, eHealthInsurance marketers are not expected to be product experts. The expertise of marketing and product knowledge have been unbundled in this new era. As Kidwell notes,

In the past, the chain of health insurance marketing typically flowed in a simple path from the insurer to its licensed insurance agents. Now, the chain involves our bundle and the value we provide through our own affiliate network. One important difference is that our affiliates are likely to be sophisticated Internet marketers who attract customer interest. We have unbundled this expertise from product expertise. Once a prospect is interested in one of our services, they can instantly talk with a licensed insurance agent, who is knowledgeable about products in the prospect's locale, via the eHealthInsurance 800 number which is prominently displayed on our Web site.

Conclusion

There are undoubtedly a host of other industries that are quickly unbundling, or will be unbundled, by go-it-alone entrepreneurs. Professional service businesses are exploding into their component functions, and the development, manufacturing, marketing, and distribution of specific products are no longer being handled by monolithic corporations. Unbundling and the go-it-alone approach to business are sweeping across the business landscape.

IMPLICATIONS OF THE HIDDEN REVOLUTION

> Never give in. Never give in. Never, never, never, never—in nothing, great or small, large or petty—never give in, except to convictions of honour and good sense.
>
> —*Winston Churchill*

How to Think about the Future of Your Business

The advances in ASPs lead to an important, perhaps counterintuitive, business perspective. There is a natural tendency to believe that almost any business will be better off with custom-designed services. Many go-it-alone entrepreneurs may even conclude that it's worth paying the cost of development. In this area, I have one absolute, unwavering piece of advice: Follow Churchill's maxim and "Never give in." Resist this temptation with all of your will!

Several years ago, I was working as a consultant to a Fortune 1000 company. The company was approached by one of the nation's leading technology firms, with whom it had a long-standing relationship, about building the company intranet—at a cost of approximately $1 million over an estimated 9 months. I was on-site for a different purpose when the president turned to me and asked what I thought about the proposal. His focus, appropriately, was on the many benefits that this intranet would bring to the firm.

My answer illustrates my perspective on how any company, small or large, should think about the services it needs. I agreed that the product produced by the technology company would, in all likelihood, meet 100% of the firm's needs. I suggested, however, that it would probably take somewhat longer than 9 months (because all software development takes longer to develop than the time budgeted). Also, the intranet would inevitably be out of date the moment it was delivered. As the state of technology advanced, the company was going to discover that it wanted even more sophisticated capabilities, so it would quickly be spending another million dollars for the next set of start-of-the art advances, with the possibility of an ongoing cycle. Because this was a custom effort, the company would also, to a certain extent, be locked into working with this provider, at least for any required support and ongoing maintenance. If another technology supplier developed something dramatically better, the company might not be able to take advantage of this breakthrough. At the same time, the company would not have an intranet for over a year, meaning lost productivity. Remember Michael Doyle's point that ASP products can often be deployed in days, as opposed to months or years.

I proposed an alternative: Approach a firm in the business of providing outsourced intranets. The Fortune 1000 company could employ an off-the-shelf solution at a fraction of the cost of the proposed custom effort through a monthly subscription and have it be up and running within 2 weeks to a month. The company would gain almost a year's productivity by accepting an out-of-the box service. Yes, it was certainly true that the intranet the company would deploy immediately would have only about 60% of the firm's wish list of features, as compared to the 100% obtained through a custom program. But in all likelihood, one year later (when the custom intranet would finally be installed), the out-of-the-box outsourced program would have added features so that it would meet 80% of the firm's needs. And 6 months after that, the added features in the subscription offering would probably offer 150% of what the firm was specifying as its needs today. Finally, when something goes wrong with an ASP, it can be fixed at the provider's site, because the service is provided to firms remotely via the Internet. It is not hosted on-site. This can lead to far easier maintenance. If something goes wrong with custom software—and it inevitably does—the developer typically must dispatch a team to the user's site, figure out what is wrong with the unique code, and then fix it. That's a far more time-consuming, costly, and disruptive process.

Providers of specialized outsourced services must constantly be working to make their offerings better, to continually earn their clients' business. Anyone who has worked with such services has seen this phenomenon. Custom products are likely to be expensive and delayed and require constant reinvestment to maintain state-of-the art capability. Aren't ASPs too good to be true? No. In fact, there is a sound economic basis for them. As noted earlier, the cost of an ASP is spread over many customers, so each customer effectively pays only a small portion of the development cost.

The very largest U.S. companies are increasingly becoming ASP users, because even they cannot keep up with the benefits offered by specialized providers. For example, Fidelity Investments is widely known as a brokerage and mutual funds provider, but an increasing percentage of the company's revenues are generated by the firm's human resources and benefits outsourcing services. This Fidelity business unit now accounts for roughly one third of the firm's total revenues, and the percentage is growing. Peter Smail, the president of Fidelity Employer Services Co., said that he expects this outsourcing business, which processes things like paychecks and health insurance, to keep growing. He anticipates that the nation's largest firms will increasingly realize they cannot match the benefits Fidelity offers clients as a result of the billions of dollars each year that the company spends on technology. "Our value proposition is that you outsource to us and we'll take care of the technology over time," he told Reuters.

Case Study: A Lesson Learned

I learned the hard way that outsourcing is the way to go. In fact, one of the most significant mistakes I made with Speed Anywhere, early in the company's life, was to spend money on what turned out to be useless software.

As the firm was being established, I was approached by a friend who wanted to join the business as a partner. We agreed that he would undertake a variety of initiatives, including building a robust consumer DSL business. At the time, there was no one place where a consumer could go to reliably check on the availability of DSL from any of the potentially multiple providers. We found a developer who could create software that would automatically perform this task the night after we received the request from the consumer. The cost would be significant but affordable if we used a large portion of the cash the business was then throwing off. Although the business had the resources to fund this effort, those funds were not earmarked as part of our budget for experiments (which was far smaller). In the early days of the company, this was been our most substantial investment, and I assumed it would pay off.

We envisioned consumers visiting the site on, say, a Tuesday and receiving an e-mail from us on Wednesday morning telling them where they could find a DSL provider in their area. The software worked, but we discovered that our basic concept was flawed. Consumers were interested in a one-stop-shopping service only if it operated in real time. They wanted to buy DSL then and there. Our subsequent research determined that consumers left our site and immediately visited other sites hoping to make an immediate purchase. The jump to a robust real-time service, with a friendly consumer interface, would have been an even greater speculative investment, so we decided instead to cut our losses and leave the consumer DSL market.

Here's the lesson: In retrospect, I see that we could have organized a small group of people to process these DSL leads at night. They could have simulated the ultimate operation of the software. So remember this: Before you get going, think creatively about ways to simulate something that may take time or money to build. It may sound silly to organize a few people to work from midnight to 3 AM, but the cost would have been far lower than what we ultimately spent on software we could not use, and we would have gained our ultimate answer far more quickly. We would have saved cash that was precious to us at that moment. And just like the Fortune 1000 firm discussed earlier, we had to wait for the software to be developed. That time, which was largely spent preparing other aspects of our failed consumer DSL business, could also have been better used.

In today's intensely competitive environment, one of the advantages go-it-alone businesses may have over their larger competitors is speed. Smaller companies can be more nimble, often acting on new insights faster than larger competitors can. The title of the national best-seller by Jason Jennings and Laurence Haughton, *It's Not the Big That Eat the Small . . . It's the Fast That Eat the Slow*, makes an important point, which the authors persuasively argue throughout the book. So here's another lesson: By seeking to design custom software, we also gave up our potential speed advantage. Using ASPs enhances your speed; using of custom software decreases it dramatically.

An additional lesson I learned is that the software would have given us a marginal advantage at best. At the time we saw a business opportunity, so did other companies with far greater programming capabilities. In essence, even if we had succeeded, we would have been quickly overtaken by our competitors, because our success would have been built on a high-cost capability that we did not control—custom software. Each effort to stay ahead of the competition would have broken the bank. To succeed, we needed to invent a business system that took advantage of low-cost resources—such as existing ASPs—and our unique marketing skills. Once we did that, a successful go-it-alone enterprise emerged.

The Rise of the Instant Company

It used to be that once you had your business idea, you needed a lengthy period for raising capital and assembling all of the necessary pieces to get up and going. Now, it's often the idea and the planning, not the physical implementation, that constrains the launch timetable. Once these conceptual aspects are in place, you can move with dramatic speed to bring the business into operation. This very low cost and easy start-up also makes it possible to quickly determine the viability of a business concept. This represents a true revolution: It's now possible to quickly test a business concept, refine the idea on the basis of live customer experience, and roll out your business in a few days for a limited investment.

There's another important point here, and it's a fundamental change: As recently as the mid-1990s, there were probably minimums, in terms of employees and cash on hand, that were required to build a sizeable company. Of course, the numbers differed greatly by industry, and by the sales volume that is considered significant in each industry. But except in a few cases, the absolute minimum number of employees needed by most businesses, to be substantial, was probably about 20. Today, that number is as low as one—you!

Case Study: Today, Anyone Can Harness the Sources of Dell's Success

In a 1998 interview in the *Harvard Business Review*, Dell Chairman and CEO Michael Dell described in detail what he viewed as the sources of his company's success—his ability to "create a business that was focused and efficient." He also described his company's philosophy of outsourcing: "As a small start-up, Dell couldn't afford to create every piece of the value chain. But more to the point, why should we want to? We concluded we'd be better off leveraging the investments others have made and focusing on delivering solutions and systems to customers."

Dell also stressed three other key points, the first being that technology, at the time of the interview, allowed for relationships and information sharing with "supplier partners in ways that just weren't possible five to ten years ago." As detailed in the outsourcing discussion in this chapter and the next one, technology has advanced since that 1998 interview according to the Rule of Decreasing Support Costs. It is now possible, through low-cost, easy-to-use plug-and-play services, for any business to effectively interact with suppliers, partners, and customers across the globe.

Dell's second point was that "it's fair to think of our companies as being virtually integrated. That allows us to focus on where we add value and to build a much larger firm much more quickly. Virtual integration means you're basically stitching together a business with partners." The value of these partners is twofold: "There are fewer things to manage, fewer things to go wrong," as Dell said, and if you set up your relationships right, you are not beholden to any single partner. This gives you the ability to negotiate price and the freedom to switch if one firm can no longer supply the best services in its category.

Finally, Dell focused on the risks posed by holding inventory. His company used daily information exchanges with suppliers in as many cases as possible, to avoid holding any inventory at all. Finished components, such as monitors from third party suppliers were ordered to match the actual demand of each day's customers. In essence, Dell figured out a way to knit together a system that minimized his use of cash and his risks of loss.

In 1998, only a large company with sophisticated information technology capabilities such as Dell could have built a business that essentially took advantage of information sharing to involve suppliers across the globe and focus on the single factor where Dell added value: understanding what the customer wanted and how those tastes changed over time, and continuously meeting those needs. At the time, a solo business that attempted to emulate Dell's approach would have found it prohibitively expensive, if not impossible.

Today, the Rule of Decreasing Support Costs has changed this calculation. Easy-to-use communications services have now made it possible for even the smallest business to easily incorporate the core ideas that Michael Dell recognized as leading to his own success: outsource everything, focus your energy relentlessly on where you add value, integrate with multiple partners so that you play a clear role in the chain of product and service creation, and hold as little cash-draining inventory as possible.

CONCLUSION

This chapter demonstrates that we are entering an era that is creating fundamentally new opportunities. As a result of ongoing advances in the creation of on-demand services, several dramatic shifts have occurred: Capabilities that were once available only to firms with large numbers of employees can now be cost-effectively harnessed by individuals. Support infrastructures that once required expensive design and investment can now be accessed on demand at low monthly subscription fees. Businesses that were of necessity operated under the same roof are now unbundling at a rapid pace. All of these changes make it possible for go-it-alone businesses to emerge and succeed. Moreover, the accelerating nature of these shifts suggests that we are just at the beginning of a new era.

4
DO WHAT YOU DO BEST

A go-it-alone business allows you to take advantage of your unique skills and do what you do best. This chapter explores how you can develop winning business ideas and assess whether these ideas appropriately match your skills. You may have a terrific business idea but be absolutely the wrong person to execute it. To succeed, your idea and the skills required to turn the idea into a success must align. This may sound self-evident. Nonetheless, many would-be entrepreneurs fail because they get caught up in the excitement of a "good" idea, without fully considering the skills needed to bring it to life.

This chapter is divided into three parts: The first—"Choosing Your Business Idea"—expands on methods for finding valuable business opportunities. The second—"What Do You Do Best?"—explains and explores the idea of core competency as it applies to go-it-alone entrepreneurs. The third—"Does Your Idea Fit with Your Core Competence?"—then describes methodologies for analyzing the fit between your unique skills and your proposed business idea.

CHOOSING YOUR BUSINESS IDEA
There's Nothing Like Experience

Earlier, in "Good Ideas Are Everywhere" on pages 14–16, I discussed a primary source of ideas for go-it-alone ventures: The solutions to problems individuals face in their own lives. Look at the problems you face in your own life, see how you solve them, and then consider whether this might be the basis for a business. Here's two examples of businesses that started in exactly this way:

- **Emoonlighter (now Guru.com)**
  The two cofounders, Professor Kannon Srinvasan of Carnegie-Mellon, and Inder Guglani, a former student of Srinvasan's, were discussing the difficulty Srinvasan was having in finding freelance talent to fulfill client requests for supplements to his consulting work. They subsequently concluded that the solution to Srinvasan's problem represented a substantial business opportunity: an online marketplace connecting freelancers with employer projects.

- **CleanAirGardening.com**
  Lars Hundley, the founder and sole employee of this online ecologically-oriented retail store for gardening was renting a home and responsible for its yard maintenance. He did not want to invest in an expensive gas-powered lawn mower. He found an inexpensive push mower at Home Depot, and subsequently wondered whether other people with an interest in the environment would share his enthusiasm for human powered mowers and related gardening items.

If you are still skeptical, here's another source. Michael Moritz of Sequoia Capital is generally regarded as one of the most astute venture capital investors of the past few decades. He has participated in funding Cisco, Yahoo!, and Apple Computer. Moritz shares my belief. While writing in a special issue of *Newsweek*, he said, "Companies often get started by people who develop a product for themselves or their close friends. It's almost accidental that their product becomes something that

millions of other people want. Almost all of our best investments have sprung from this personal impulse."

Here's one technique for finding the business ideas in your
own experience. For one month, make a note every time you are
confronted with a problem that seems ridiculous, either because
it is frustrating, or it is wasting your time, or your intuition tells
you that there has to be an easier way. If you solve one of these
problems for yourself, you may also have invented your next
career.

Other Sources of Ideas

There are several other sources of business ideas that are particularly appropriate for go-it-alone initiatives.

Where Else Would It Work?

In *Why Not?: How to Use Everyday Ingenuity to Solve Problems
Big and Small*, Barry Nalebuff, a professor at the Yale School of
Management, and Ian Ayres, a professor at the Yale Law School,
create a framework for developing innovative ideas. One component is the notion that in many cases there are solutions waiting for problems. Here, the business founder takes a concept or
technology that works in one arena and finds other areas where
it can be applied successfully. One example of this kind of innovation is the development of the low-cost spinning toothbrush:
the SpinBrush.

John Osher is the successful entrepreneur who, as discussed
earlier, adopted "Determination" as his personal motto. He
developed and sold the Spin Pop, a spinning lollipop with a toy
attached. While walking through the aisles of a drugstore,
Osher realized that this same technology could be applied to the
development of a *low-cost* automated toothbrush. This insight led

to the development of the SpinBrush, which Procter & Gamble subsequently purchased for $475 million. In discussing his success with the publication *Knowledge at Wharton*, Osher noted the importance of using existing technology: "Our advantage was that we were trying to design up from 80 cents, while everybody else was trying to design down from $79."

Business models that are successful in one industry may also inspire successful innovations in other industries. The now-familiar Internet-based mortgage lending model, where multiple lenders compete for each consumer's business, has been applied to a variety of consumer and business-to-business comparison shopping arenas, including life insurance, car buying, phone services, broadband, and health insurance.

Where Can Unbundling Occur?

As discussed earlier, the unbundling of specialized activities from larger companies is one inevitable consequence of the growth of the Internet. These activities may be functions performed today in large corporations, or they may be services that have been bundled into the activities of professional service firms. Look for particular functions that today are undertaken as part of a larger or bundled activity that can be broken out, with a specialized firm handling them better, faster, or more cheaply.

"I Can Do It Better"

Wyck Hay, a cofounder of herbal tea maker Celestial Seasonings, decided to create KaBoom Beverages after he sampled Red Bull, a drink imported from Austria. As detailed earlier, he believed he could create a tastier, healthier product at a lower cost. In essence, he launched a product in an area that had a demonstrated customer appeal, and improved on it to cater to

the needs of a specific market segment—in this case, the population that wants a healthier, less artificial drink.

Most new products or services are, in reality, incremental
improvements on existing ones. In considering this option, there
are two important questions to keep in mind: First, put yourself in
the place of your target customers. Is your potential new product
or service sufficiently better, either in the features it offers or the
cost involved, so that customers will shift to your offering from
whatever they are using today? Second, what happens to your proposed business if existing participants in this arena quickly match
your improvement in response to the threat of your offering? It's a
tremendous plus for your business opportunity if you have a valid
reason to believe this type of fast competitive response is unlikely,
or impossible, in the business area you are assessing.

Focus on a Dysfunctional Industry

In its 2003 annual ranking of the fastest-growing small public
companies, *Fortune Small Business* magazine concluded that
inefficient industries or industries in flux are good places to
build a supercharged company. Thomas Cigarran, the cofounder
of American Healthways, which ranked number one on the
magazine's list, noted that "health care is a mess, and we'll just
keep focusing on what's not working." Cigarran told the magazine that great business opportunities arise in industries that are
not functioning properly. "There are just so many opportunities
to make this sector more functional," he says. This book repeatedly stresses the importance of focus in creating a go-it-alone
business. In a dysfunctional industry, this means finding a very
specific, meaningful problem (perhaps one that you or a friend
has experienced) and developing a useful solution. Plus, it can't
be too far ahead of the customer or the industry, as detailed in
Chapter 2, "Principles for Success."

Look for Unrecognized Value

Michael Loeb, the cofounder of the highly successful Synapse Group (www.Synapsegroupinc.com), notes that "one man's garbage is another man's treasure." Synapse succeeded, in part, by turning credit-card billing statements into a valuable sales medium. "No one had ever regarded this as a true communications medium or optimized it," he says. Start by identifying under-used assets, and find a way to bring value to the asset owners on an outsourced basis. The fascinating story of how the Synapse Group realized this objective is detailed on pages 167–170.

Imagine Potential Pricing Innovations

Many businesses are held back because of the way they set prices. Fees based on hourly rates—which are open-ended—as compared to flat rates often discourage purchases. All types of upfront fees, with no guarantee of results, similarly discourage firms from trying new services. Companies that have figured out how to eliminate the risks for the customer in their pricing systems, while still earning a profit, have proven to be solid innovators. In fact, a particularly useful finding of the research and interviews for this book is the significant extent to which businesses built on extreme outsourcing employed strategies related to pricing innovation. Many such businesses found approaches to pricing that worked for the entrepreneurs and made it incredibly easy for prospective customers to say yes.

Businesspeople are always concerned about the potential, unchecked cost of service work that is billed by the hour. As detailed on pages 106-108, a central component of 1–800-MYLOGO's (www.1800mylogo.com) initial success was the development of a flat-rate package that served the client's needs and allowed the company to make efficient use of its time. Similarly, Michael

Loeb's decision at the Synapse Group to offer a flat rate for access to credit card statements (detailed in Chapter 10) immediately reinvented the decision for the credit card operator, as compared with more typical requests, to pay owners a percentage of the money earned or generated. The success of Emoonlighter (now Guru.com) accelerated when its pricing system focused on charging professionals a percentage of their fees for completed assignments instead of charging corporations for participating in the marketplace. This pricing mechanism encouraged corporations to test using the marketplace without risk, because they only incurred costs after a professional successfully completed a specific assignment.

This certainly suggests that you may want to focus on a business that has trouble attracting customers because of pricing uncertainty. The goal is to create a pricing system that makes sense to the customer and permits a far easier yes than what already exists. Of course, to create a winning business it's not enough to simply establish a fixed fee. This may be a quick route to losing your shirt. You need to find a way to limit your risk or perform sufficient tests so that you know that you will make money on these fixed-fee activities, at least in the majority of cases.

Look for Opportunities Deemed Too Small by Large Companies

Most large companies won't pursue new initiatives unless they have the chance to make a meaningful contribution to the bottom line. As a consequence, billion-dollar firms may identify and choose not to pursue million dollar prospects. A June 2004 *Business Week* cover story on the 100 best small companies noted, for example, that "In the drive to market, some opportunities are always left behind. These tasty scraps are meat and potatoes for some Hot Growth companies." How do you find out about these abandoned opportunities? If you have an expertise in a specific industry, a careful reading of the trade press is one likely source of information.

Consider Turning a Product into a Service

The discussion of ASPs in this book shows the ongoing evolution of software products into monthly subscription services. Many of these are go-it-alone businesses. Similarly, Michael Loeb at the Synapse Group, built his business, in part, on transforming the delivery of magazines from a product (with multiple bills appearing in the mailbox every few months) to a service (with payment via the customer's credit card), which appealed to a specific group of buyers. Are there ways you can group existing products, or reshape them, to form a service that provides higher value to consumers?

Look for Opportunities to Provide Outsourcing

Outsourcing of all types of functions, as detailed throughout this book, is unquestionably a growing trend. In part, this phenomenon is fueled by the unbundling arising from the growth of the Internet. Many go-it-alone firms provide outsourced services: The highly focused, relentlessly repeatable characteristics of such businesses make them desirable opportunities for go-it-alone entrepreneurs. Once again, the best way to locate a valuable outsourcing opportunity is likely to be your own experience: Take note if you find yourself doing something time-consuming and wondering why there's no existing business that makes the task involved a lot easier.

Use the Web Site for This Book

The contents of the Web site (www.BruceJudson.com) for this book are described on page 205. The site will, among other things, post thought-provoking stories of how other go-it-alone entrepreneurs came up with the ideas for their businesses. Additional materials associated with choosing a business idea will also be posted at the site.

WHAT DO YOU DO BEST?

The do-what-you-do-best approach to choosing a business idea clearly suggests that there is an abundance of good ideas for go-it-alone entrepreneurs. Indeed, the use of the word *choosing* is deliberate: It implies one of many, as opposed to *finding*, which might imply something rare or hard to locate. However, it's possible that you have a terrific idea but are not well suited to carry out the associated business, particularly if you are planning a solo business. Once you have a prospective idea, the first question you need to consider is your own skills: Will the business idea take advantage of what you do best?

The Idea of Core Competence

At the center of a successful go-it-alone business is the central skill or expertise of the founder. The application of this expertise is what ultimately makes the business a success. An essential element in establishing your business is to identify the reason your business will be a success and articulate for yourself the skills that will be involved.

Today, management theorists typically refer to the central skill of an organization as its core competence; a term that is discussed at length by Gary Hamel and C. K. Prahalad in their book *Competing for the Future*. They persuasively argue that the long-term success of any business depends on the "potentiality that is released" when it appropriately focuses on exploiting its core competence. The authors define a core competence as "a bundle of skills and technologies that enables a company to provide a particular benefit to customers." This definition, which is appropriate for a Fortune 500 firm, can be adapted for our purposes: The core competence of a go-it-alone firm typically lies in the skill or skills that enable the firm to provide a benefit to customers. Or: It is what you do best that allows you to create something that is valuable to a customer.

It's particularly useful to take note of the other central ideas presented by Hamel and Prahalad. First, the idea of core competence is in part meant to encourage focus. They note that "there must be some sense of what activities really contribute to long-term corporate prosperity." They also suggested that "to be considered a core competence a skill must meet three tests":

- **Customer value:** "A core competence must make a disproportionate contribution to customer-perceived value." In essence, a core competence must be a central reason a customer chooses the products or services of a specific company. (Example: Mr. Trademark's expertise in trademark searches.)
- **Competitor differentiation:** A core competence "must also be competitively unique." This means that it is a capability that helps to set the business apart from its competition. (Example: Mr. Trademark provides searches faster and lower-priced than competitors.)
- **Extendability:** From the perspective of "tomorrow's markets," a core competence should lead a company to imagine "an array of new products or services issuing from the competence." (Example: Mr. Trademark starts assisting with trademark applications in addition to performing searches.)

Core Competencies in Action

As you consider a go-it-alone initiative, the central point here is to have a clear understanding of the skill—the core competence—that will underlie the success of the business in question.

Not only will this central skill allow you to attract customers and provide something that customers want, but also will be what your support system of ASPs work to leverage.

Surprisingly, your core competencies may not be what they seem. They may create customer value, but they may not be visible to the customer—they are not necessarily the end product or service. Hamel and Prahalad vividly make this point: "Few computer users could tell you much about the competencies that support the user-friendly interface of a Macintosh, but they do know that the computer is refreshingly easy to use."

When Shannan Bishop of Gourmet Gatherings was asked what she viewed as central to the success of the firm, her answer wasn't what you might expect. She believes that both she and her partner are "high-energy entertainers." In this respect, they have used the catering business as a way to channel their enthusiasm for providing an engaging experience to an audience.

The example of Gourmet Gatherings is useful as you think about how you take a core competence and turn it into a business. In essence, you are looking for a platform that lends itself to creating value where you do what you do best. As Hamel and Prahalad point out, the core skill that drives a business success may not be obvious: You may need to carefully "look under the hood" to find the skills that will drive a business to success.

DOES YOUR IDEA FIT WITH YOUR CORE COMPETENCE?

You may identify a great idea, but that does not in itself mean it is a great business idea for you. To succeed, you will almost certainly need to achieve excellence in whatever you undertake. This, in turn, will require that you have the opportunity to leverage what you do best. Indeed, superb execution is absolutely critical to the success of a go-it-alone venture. Indeed, I would argue that you are far more likely to succeed if you superbly execute a mediocre idea than if you execute a superb idea in a mediocre way.

It is therefore essential that you both identify your core competence and then spend considerable time analyzing whether the business idea you are considering will allow you to leverage this core skill.

Identifying Your Core Competence

A full examination of how you determine your core competence is beyond the scope of this book. However, what follows is an attempt to summarize some excellent thinking that has been done on this subject.

Methodology 1: Find Your Greatest Strength

If you are in the process of analyzing your skills, take a look at *Now, Discover Your Strengths*, by Marcus Buckingham and Donald Clifton. These authors start from a premise that is similar to mine. They note that most businesses often operate on the belief that each person's greatest potential for growth is in his or her arenas of greatest weakness. They believe that instead, organizations should recognize that "each person's talents are enduring and unique," and that "each person's greatest potential for growth is in the areas of his or her greatest strength." As stated earlier, they forcefully suggest that "the real tragedy in life is not that each of us doesn't have enough strengths, it's that we fail to use the ones we have."

These authors distinguish between strengths and talents: A strength is "consistent, near perfect performance in an activity." An example the authors cite is Cole Porter, whose "ability to carve the perfect lyric was a strength. His attempts at writing believable characters and plots were not." Within this framework, Buckingham and Clifton develop "principles of living a strong life":

> First, for an activity to be a strength you must be able to do it consistently. And this implies that it is a predictable part of your performance. . . . The acid test of a strength? The ability is a strength if you can fathom yourself doing it repeatedly, happily, and successfully.
>
> Second, you do not have to have strength in every aspect of your role in order to excel. . . . [No one] is blessed with the "perfect hand," . . . That excellent performers must be well rounded is one of the most pervasive myths we hope to dispel in this book. When we studied them, excellent performers were rarely well rounded. On the contrary, they were sharp.
>
> Third, you will excel only by maximizing your strengths, never by fixing your weaknesses. . . . [Excellent performers] found ways to manage around their weaknesses, thereby freeing them up to hone their strengths to a sharper point . . .

Buckingham and Clifton then move on to discussing talents: "Your talents, your strongest synaptic connections, are the most important raw materials for strength building. Identify your most powerful talents, hone them with skills and knowledge, and you will be on your way to living the strong life." They suggest several strategies for identifying your real talents, including these:

- "Monitor your spontaneous, top-of-mind reactions to the situations you encounter. These top-of-mind reactions provide the best trace of your talents. They reveal the location of strong mental connections."

- "Yearnings reveal the presence of a talent, particularly when they are felt early in life."
- "Rapid learning offers another trace of talent . . . You start to learn a new skill—in the context of a new job, a new challenge, or a new environment—and immediately your brain seems to light up as if a whole bank of switches were suddenly flicked to 'on.'"
- "Satisfactions provide the last clue to talent. . . . Your strongest synaptic connections are designed so that when you use them you feel good."

Buckingham and Clifton advise that "Spontaneous reactions, yearnings, rapid learning, and satisfactions will all help you to detect the traces of your talents. As you rush through your busy life, try to step back, quiet the wind whipping past your ears, and listen for these clues. They will help you to zero in on your talents." Once you have identified your talents you can start *"to capitalize on your strengths, whatever they may be, and manage around your weaknesses, whatever they may be."*

Methodology 2: Find Your Source of Personal Energy

An alternative but strikingly similar method for assessing your core skills is suggested by Dr. Kathleen Hall, the author of *Alter Your Life: How to Turn Everyday Activities into Spiritually Rewarding Experiences.* When she was writing, Dr. Hall was struggling with how to express the idea of purpose and meaning in work—what most of us would call our individual passion. After a great deal of thought, she decided that *energy* was the answer. Dr. Hall concluded that "whenever you do something that makes you feel great, that releases energy, you have tapped into what you should be doing."

With this idea in mind, Dr. Hall devised a simple exercise

for assessing your core competence. Almost every entrepreneur will tell you that success requires a passion for what you are doing. Dr. Hall suggests that you think back on the times when you have done something that released a surge of energy. These energy surges mean that you are acting in concert with what we are calling your core competence—the unique skill or passion that is what you do best, and that you find gratifying.

Laura Walker, president and CEO of WNYC Radio, describes this kind of energy release. She says that when she was a child, "my father and I used to listen to jazz together on the radio. I have just always had this incredibly strong feeling that the medium was important, so every day that I help to realize this vision is exciting to me. I am just passionate about building this important outlet for news, ideas, and culture."

Play to Your Strengths

The importance of the fit between your business idea and your core competence cannot be overstated. Playing to your core strength is important for two reasons. First, as a solo entrepreneur, you must achieve excellence in what you do on your own. You are far more likely to realize this goal if you are inherently talented in the arena you choose to enter. Second, we typically enjoy the things in which we have a natural affinity, so working in the area of your core competence is also likely to generate the energy and passion that will further drive your new business toward success.

Many people make the mistake of thinking that because they have a good idea, they can execute it. In fact, you may have a terrific idea with extraordinary commercial potential, but you may be absolutely the wrong person to build the associated business, particularly in a solo effort. Jeff Bezos, the founder of Amazon.com and *Time*'s Person of the Year for 1999, puts it this way: "One of the huge mistakes people make is [trying] to force an interest on themselves. . . . If you're really interested in medicine, and you decide you're going to become an Internet entrepreneur because it looks like everybody else is doing well, then that's probably not going to work. You don't choose your passions, your passions choose you."

There are many examples of go-it-alone entrepreneurs who have succeeded because they have aligned their core business activities with their core skills: Mitch York, whose activities as a Maui Wowi franchisee are detailed in Chapter 7 (pages 141–143), exercises his tremendous marketing creativity to make the business a success. Sherman Eisner, who founded A&E Home Security Company for do-it-yourselfers, describes himself as "mechanically inclined" and has a unique ability "to envision the problems a customer may be facing" in self-installation, so he can provide unparalleled phone support. The founder of 1–800-MYLOGO, David Tartamella, had an unusual and very strong interest in corporate identities and the design of logos from early childhood. What's exciting is the way he has turned this interest into a worldwide business. (See The Art of the Repeatable Business System, pages 106–108.)

Do You Need to Be an Expert?

One question that naturally arises is the value of subject expertise in building your business. Do you need to be an expert to make your business a success?

When you develop a business idea, you may see that it fits with your core skills and has real value to potential customers. You may not, however be an expert in the business area involved. Indeed, many go-it-alone entrepreneurs start with limited expertise but have the capacity to learn rapidly. This facility is a direct result of the alignment between the business idea and their talents (as postulated by Buckingham and Clifton). So the answer is both no, at the start of the business, and yes, for the business to move forward. The pattern that seems to repeat itself over and over again is that the go-it-alone entrepreneur has an insight that can create value and that fits with his or her core competence. This insight is enough to fuel a successful start to the business. But once the business gets off the ground, the entrepreneur does need to become something of an expert in his or her operating arena in order to successfully expand the range of product offerings and optimize the overall performance of the business.

The evidence suggests that expertise in an area that matches your unique skills can be learned and should not be an intimidating barrier to moving forward. When an area fits with your core competence, it releases tremendous energy and learning tends to come swiftly and sometimes effortlessly. Your natural talents make you an intuitive learner in this area.

5

HOW TO CREATE YOUR BUSINESS SYSTEM

Is it really possible to magnify a skill into a substantial, thriving business? Yes. This chapter tells you how, following these principles:

- Leverage your core competence through relentless repeatability.
- Identify the important metrics.
- Make time work for you—instead of against you.
- Take advantage of the benefits of scale.
- Follow the 60% Rule.
- Build for flexibility.
- Make your own luck.

LEVERAGE YOUR CORE COMPETENCE THROUGH RELENTLESS REPEATABILITY

Chapter 1 discussed the essential need for relentless repeatability. This repeatable system is built around your core competence: what you do best. It is the basic formula for your business: leverage and extreme outsourcing then allow you to magnify your core competence into a business that can grow without limits. One of the central attributes of successful go-it-alone businesses is that they find creative ways to make almost any activity relentlessly repeatable.

Case Study: The Art of the Repeatable Business System

1-800-MYLOGO (www.1800mylogo.com) is one example of a business that uses leverage and repeatable systems. The firm, which was established in 1996, creates professionally designed corporate identity logos at package prices ranging in 2004 from $199 to $499. The target market for the service is small and medium-size businesses. The company's services have been recommended by a host of authoritative media entities, including *Entrepreneur* magazine and *Inc.* magazine. The company was profitable almost immediately—and was established without any outside capital. What's remarkable about 1-800-MYLOGO is that the central business fundamentally involves graphic artists. It almost seems oxymoronic to use the word *art* and *systems* in the same sentence, which is, of course, why this is such an interesting example.

The way 1-800-MYLOGO works is this: Customers log onto the Web site, read compelling sales material, and decide whether to purchase one of several packages. Customers who make a purchase fill out a detailed questionnaire about the type of logo they are looking for. The questions range from where the logo will be used to colors that the customer prefers to qualitative issues involving the purpose and image of the firm.

Each package explicitly describes the process the firm uses in working with the customer. The lowest-priced service at a total fee of $199, the Ultra Logo Design Package includes six original concepts of the logo, in an unlimited number of colors, with designs by three different artists. In an easy-to-use secure access area of the Web site, the company posts these designs. The customer then chooses a favorite design and posts comments. The company works with the customer in a back-and-forth process of comments and revisions until the customer is satisfied with the completed design. At the outset, the company limited the back-and-forth process to three rounds of comments, and customers were told this in purchasing the package. This was a brilliant mechanism for ensuring that the company could profitably deliver a quality product at a flat fee, without charging by the hour. Indeed, this original pricing innovation is probably one of the central reasons for the firm's initial success. Businesses are always concerned about the cost of open-ended commitments, and the firm found a profitable way to provide a quality service at a fixed price. After several years of experience, the company modified this policy to allow additional minor revisions, but the critical elements that allowed the company to get going are what are particularly noteworthy here.

Here's why the overall approach of 1-800-MYLOGO is so compelling: While we tend to think of graphic arts as a local service business, the company has taken a piece of the graphic arts business, developed a specialty, and systematized it. Moreover, 1-800-MYLOGO has addressed the four central problems that every service business must deal with: (1) the unpaid time and effort involved in selling the service, (2) balancing custom expertise with the time involved, (3) getting and keeping happy customers while limiting the number of customers who will never be satisfied (and will chew up valuable time and resources with endless demands), and (4) the customer's desire to pay a flat fee (as opposed to an hourly rate) for a product that can be difficult for the company to assess ahead of time.

How does the company do it? First, the company focuses on what it does best: create logos. Customers are recruited through a terrific Web site, advertising, well-orchestrated publicity, repeat business, and word of mouth. Second, the Web site acts as the salesperson. The company avoids the high costs associated with salespeople. Third, the initial "three revisions and you're done" limitation was a superb way of managing customer expectations and engaging the customer. By clearly articulating this policy upfront, 1-800-MYLOGO logo forced customers to take every revision seriously. Customers knew they had to think carefully before they used the artists' time because they would have only so many opportunities. Finally, the three-revisions approach realistically weeded out undesirable, and ultimately unprofitable, customers. The company initially limited its risk because it assumed that if a customer would not be happy after three revisions, he or she would never be happy (and should either pay more or work with someone else).

Here's a valuable takeaway thought from the 1-800-MYLOGO story: If a specific graphic arts activity can be set up as a repeatable and profitable business, then with enough creativity and thought, you can probably do the same for almost any service.

IDENTIFY THE IMPORTANT METRICS

Most successful businesses are repeatable formulas, because there are typically a few relationships that determine the overall success of the business. It's vitally important to identify these crucial leverage points, so that you can focus your attention and efforts on improving them. In *Profit from the Core: Growth Strategy in an Era of Turbulence*, Chris Zook persuasively makes a related point. He argues that most businesses fail to fully realize the potential strength of their core functions and that a greater focus on the high-leverage points (which yield 80% of the benefits of the business) will inevitably lead to greater success.

Within the context of Speed Anywhere, here are the implications of these ideas. In this business, I am paid for leads that successfully translate into sales. If I send 1,000 prospects to a company and only 5 convert to customers, it is these 5 for which I am paid. The other leads have absolutely no value (and may even have a negative value because the sales force of the telecommunications company is wasting its time on fruitless sales efforts). As a consequence, the business has five basic numbers that I watch:

1. The number of people that visit the Web site offering the service
2. My marketing cost to bring a potential prospect to the site (my cost per potential lead)
3. My conversion rate at the site (the percentage of people who fill out the on-site form and ask for quotes as compared to the total number of visitors)
4. My conversion rate of prospects submitted to companies (the percentage of submitted leads that actually results in broadband purchases for which I am compensated)
5. The average compensation I receive for each sale (my average value of a sold customer)

With these five metrics, I can in fact reduce the business to a simple mathematical formula. What's important here is that each of these areas provides a window into how I can influence the profits of the business. Two obvious places that influence profits are items 1 and 5 (basic costs and basic compensation). However, it's often the less obvious—but equally important—leverage points—that are frequently the sources of business success.

If I want to double the profits of the business, I have a range of options. Items 1 and 5 suggest that I can attempt to lower my basic marketing costs by one-half (which, in an optimized system, is likely to be hard) or I can negotiate with my affiliated broadband providers to double my compensation (which sounds like a tough sell). Alternatively, I can look at some of the internal measures of how the business is functioning. For example, if 5% of the visitors to the site decide to sign up for the service, my profits also double if I can raise this number to 10% (assuming they are prospects of the same quality). Doubling this conversion rate has exactly the same impact on profits as cutting my marketing costs in half. I am now paying only 50% of what I was previously paying for a lead that is submitted to a telecommunications firm. Because this conversion rate was entirely a product of my business system, I concluded that it would be the lowest-cost high-leverage point for increasing profits. I embarked on an effort to increase the efficiency of conversion at the site. It was far easier to work at improving this leverage point—which was entirely within my control—than, for example, to convince providers to double my compensation for each sale.

Dr. Ross Jaffe, the health care venture capitalist, believes that entrepreneurs need to understand what he calls "the physics of business"—the key forces that drive the sales and profits in a venture. He stresses that the most successful entrepreneurs are people who have an idea or technology but also understand how to put the system together, and where they should spend time and effort to drive the bottom line. The above discussion of Speed Anywhere and the search to identify the high-leverage point where specific efforts can yield the greatest impact on profits is one example of this type of thinking.

In *Good to Great*, Jim Collins makes an even stronger point with regard to the importance of metrics and what he calls the "denominator" question. Collins found that "every good-to-great company attained the notion of a single 'economic denominator'":

> Think about it in terms of the following question: *If you could pick one and only one ratio—profit per x (or, in the social sector, cash flow per x)—to systematically increase over time, what x would have the greatest and most sustainable impact on your economic engine?* We learned this single question leads to profound insight into the inner workings of an organization's economics . . .
>
> Do you need to have a single denominator? No, but pushing for a single denominator tends to produce a better insight than letting yourself off the hook with three or four denominators. The denominator question

serves as a mechanism to force deeper understanding of
the key drivers in your economic engine . . .

As you start to set up your business, you must be able to
identify the central metrics that will determine your success or
failure. This is critical for several reasons:

- **If you can't yet identify these points, you're not ready to
start the business in earnest.**
- **Prioritizing your time and energy is of major importance.**
You will not have the time to constantly examine every cost
and every relationship, so you must have some highly reliable
quick measures that tell you how the business is doing—and
serve as early warning signs of trouble. You are far more likely
to spot a building problem faster through one of your metrics
than through the overall profit measures you use.
- **If you don't get the metrics right, there's a good chance
you'll lead your start-up to ruin.** In *Why Smart Executives
Fail and What You Can Learn from Their Mistakes*, Sydney
Finkelstein, a professor at Dartmouth's Tuck School of Business Administration, found that one prescription for disaster
is company executives who consistently look at the "wrong
scoreboard" and emphasize poor measures of success.
- **You need to get the right focus.** By understanding the
physics of your business, you are likely to spot the places
where you can apply your energy and have a major impact
on your profits.

MAKE TIME WORK FOR YOU INSTEAD OF AGAINST YOU

"Once we became profitable, we were no longer fighting time.
We turned time to our advantage," says Inder Guglani, CEO
of the company now called Guru.com. He believes that *"Most*

businesses don't fail; they simply run out of time." The classic start-up races against time—either to reach cash flow break-even before the company runs out of money or to make sufficient progress so that the company can convince additional investors to fund the next round of corporate development.

If you can create a business that is profitable from the start, or quickly thereafter, you have taken the greatest enemy of any start-up—time—and turned it from a foe into an ally. Once you are self-sustaining, there is, of course, an ongoing pressure to develop the business. Nonetheless, you can focus on building the business appropriately, as opposed to being constantly concerned about the very viability of the enterprise.

The basic formula of limited investment, extreme outsourcing, and live customers before you give up your day job is geared toward making the business cash flow positive as quickly as possible, which is the first real step in establishing long-term viability.

Case Study: David Bests Goliath in Building a Market for Freelance Employees

One example of a go-it-alone firm that succeeded by focusing on building a cash-positive sustainable business is Emoonlighter.com. In any story about the freelance work space in 1998, Emoonlighter.com, which was started in the basement of Inder Guglani and subsequently raised $400,000, would unquestionably have been described as David. Guru.com, which raised over $63 million dollars, would be the story's Goliath. Ultimately, Emoonlighter.com's disciplined approach succeeded, and in 2003 the company bought the assets of Guru.com, which exhausted its full $63 million dollars in funding. With the purchase, Emoonlighter.com adopted the moniker of the better known Guru.com, and it now operates under this name.

When Guglani cofounded Emoonlighter.com (under the original name A2Zmoonlighter.com) it had three employees. The $400,000 came from angel investors. The company achieved profitability in November 2001. As the company was changing its name to Guru.com in 2004, it had just nine employees.

Several elements of the company's development are noteworthy applications of the ideas expressed here:

- Guglani believes that his company succeeded because of its focus on achieving profitability. "We outmaneuvered our competitors by concentrating on profitability. We focused on achieving the shortest path to profitability while our competitors tried to outspend one another to capitalize on the first-mover advantage," he says. "In some ways, once we achieved profitability we were free to take more risks." Guru.com is now the world's largest online marketplace for freelance talent.

- Emoonlighter.com has remained flexible. It started with the idea of providing existing workers an opportunity to earn extra income in their free time: It was, in effect, a matchmaking service for people who wanted to moonlight on weekends and at night. This made sense in the full-employment economy that existed at the height of the dot-com boom. Later, when the full-time job market softened, Emoonlighter.com shifted to serve as a matchmaking service for people looking for full-time projects. As discussed earlier, successful businesses often end up making money in related but different areas from the ones they anticipated at launch.

- The firm has succeeded with such a small employee base by outsourcing as much as possible. Guglani notes that he anticipates that he will outsource more functions when "his employees are sufficiently experienced to manage the outsourced provider. We need to understand it in-house first," he says.

- Guglani is emphatic about testing and learning from customers. In this regard, he describes himself as risk averse. Nothing is implemented without relentless experimentation and customer feedback. "We test and then we retest," he says. "And the market can change, which means we can't assume what worked at one time will continue to work. The biggest challenge in doing business day to day is to keep the patience and discipline that has brought us to this point. Each day we fight the urge to dive into untested waters and quench our thirst to accelerate."

- Emoonlighter.com's success accelerated when it changed its pricing model to take a percentage of the revenue earned by freelancers from jobs it helped them secure. Once again, this is a common theme that runs through this book: Start-ups often test a variety of business and pricing models, and their success is often built on finding the right innovation in this area. They find the payment system that makes the most sense for each party to the transaction.

Blake Barker, an entrepreneur writing in an article distributed by *Business Week Online* about his experiences, echoed the importance of ensuring that time is not working against you. Indeed, Barker suggests that the central business model innovation that made his firm a success, a U.S. Department of Agriculture (USDA) designation, took at least a year to earn. But because he carefully analyzed his market prior to launching his business, Texas Beef and Pork Company (www.texacan.com), he understood that this would be the basis for the competitive advantage of his effort, and he built sufficient time into his launch schedule.

> . . . you must take the time to understand the market, the competition, and, above all, to reinforce your unique selling proposition. At Texacan, we wholesale and retail specialty meats. Period. That's what we do. . . .

One of Texacan's differentiators is the safety and consistency of the product. For me, the best way to communicate that message to potential customers is through USDA designation. It took me nearly a year to learn how the USDA works, how to get an inspector into my facility, and how to design my production process in a way to earn the UDS stamp of approval.

Know your competition. I had the luxury of that year because I gave it to myself. Yes, I took a cut in pay to get it. But taking the time to master my differentiator enabled me to hit the ground running when I launched my company. . . . *That was only possible through the investment of time.* [Emphasis is mine.]

TAKE ADVANTAGE OF THE BENEFITS OF SCALE

One of the central questions to ask yourself as you set up your business is: Does it have the potential to achieve the benefits of scale? First, it's important to clarify exactly what this means. *Scale* is a somewhat overused word that can mean different things in different contexts. Earlier, this book discussed the importance of businesses that scale. In that context, *scale* refers to businesses that can grow relatively easily, meaning that with growth, you won't need to hire lots of additional people, that you can handle the workload without a loss in quality, and that an increased volume of business won't overwhelm you with increased complexity.

The phrase *benefits of scale* is different. This refers to the extra values businesses typically realize when they reach a certain size. To fully understand the benefits of scale, there is nothing like experience. I found that the day-to-day practical value of scale, and in building Speed Anywhere and Health Plans Today, exceeded all of my expectations. Each day, in a hundred intangible ways, scale matters. The lesson is clear: Part of building a successful go-it-alone business is to choose a niche where

you can achieve scale. Do you need to be the biggest entrant to achieve scale? No. Must you dominate your niche? No. Here's a good rule of thumb: You want to set up a business that is big enough so that your company *really matters* to other people in your business chain.

My experience and research suggests the following analysis of how companies benefit by achieving scale:

- **Scale means better access to anyone who matters to your business.** From senior executives at telecommunications companies to account executives supervising advertising programs at search engines, my ability to reach the right people and get things done escalated dramatically as the business grew in size. Whether you are trying to propose new ways of doing things or to solve problems that are part of your ongoing business, you are far more likely to see your phone calls answered and returned, and to get the ear of decision makers when you are a meaningful source of business to them.

- **Achieving scale almost always means that you will earn more.** Most companies, for example, expect to pay more per unit (through bonuses, incentives, and other arrangements) to their top producers. In fact, many companies set their base compensation lower than their actual profits permit, since they anticipate that significant producers will negotiate for higher fees.

- **As you grow, wholesalers and suppliers start to approach you.** Whether or not you choose to do business with them, this provides a perspective on the wholesale pricing that becomes available for your purchases. In a *SmartMoney* article on eBay merchants, the magazine persuasively makes this point:

But your work isn't done yet. Prepare to woo your wholesalers. It was months before Steve Weinberg, a 43-

year-old El Dorado Hills, CA, eBay entrepreneur, lined up wholesalers for his consumer electronics business.

"You can go to Kodak and say you want to buy direct, and they say, 'How many million do you want?'" he says. Distributors, meanwhile, saw him as a small-time unknown entity. Finally, after hundreds of cold calls to wholesalers, Weinberg found a few willing to sell digital cameras to him as long as he paid up front. Now, with his monthly revenues exceeding $25,000, distributors are calling him, eager for his business.

- **As you grow larger, your per unit costs decrease.** Suppliers will start to offer you volume discounts and other arrangements that lower your cost per unit. As you build scale, your per unit costs for any repeatable activity will almost surely decline over time for a second important reason: With increased experience, you will inevitably find more ways to perform repeatable tasks with fewer steps and increased efficiency.

- **An important value of scale also occurs in marketing.** As a firm becomes more substantial, it is far more likely to generate positive publicity (assuming it seeks this publicity). Both Gourmet Gatherings and 1-800-MYLOGO have been profiled or recommended in numerous national magazines. To achieve this kind of invaluable publicity, the firms had to offer a terrific service and reach a certain critical mass. Magazines and newspapers are unlikely to cover a new business, no matter how innovative, that has not demonstrated its value to a significant number of buyers.

- **As you grow, new and often unexpected revenue opportunities start to appear.** After Speed Anywhere served over 15,000 customers, I could develop revenues related to sponsorship of a monthly e-mail newsletter. To attract sponsorship interest, the newsletter had to reach an audience of a meaningful size. Similarly, Laura Walker, the CEO of WNYC Radio, notes that as the station's listening audience grew, "We were able to develop all kinds of new, innovative forms of underwriting and other revenue streams that were only possible because of our larger size."

- **With growth, other businesses care about your success.** Once you reach a size where you matter to others in the supply chain, you have become a valuable asset to these firms. This may mean that there are opportunities to create financial arrangements that reflect the benefits of success with your business. You may, for example, be able to negotiate a wide variety of benefits such as faster payments, vendor financing, and loans secured by anticipated receivables.

As you think through setting up the business you want, seek to establish one that will allow you to achieve scale. Your enterprise doesn't need to be the largest business on the block, but there are very real benefits to businesses that achieve a certain size or critical mass, and these benefits contribute to longevity and sustainability.

FOLLOW THE 60% RULE

> The perfect is the enemy of the good.
>
> —*Voltaire*

The developer of a go-it-alone venture must have an obsession with time. What I call The 60% Rule, is essentially all about how you spend your time. In its simplest form, *the 60% Rule holds that the best solution is to automate everything except the core focus of your business, using inexpensive plug-and-play services, even when these services only provide 60% of the functionality you want.* This means, for example, that it is better to inexpensively automate an activity than to do it yourself, even if the results of the automated service are only 60% as good they might be if you did them by hand. Similarly, this rule incorporates the ideas detailed in Chapter 2, "Principles for Success," that it almost never makes sense to pay for the design of custom software when a lower-cost but inferior solution is publicly available.

It's actually hard to describe the tremendous power that results from following this seemingly simple rule. In fact, following these precepts will in all likelihood be essential to the success of any business started by an individual with limited capital. Here's why the 60% Rule is so important: As I started to investigate the capabilities of inexpensive ASP platforms for Speed Anywhere, one element kept resurfacing: I found that each service could typically meet only 60% of my needs. I was also absolutely convinced that if I devoted my own time to the service each ASP was handling, I could easily do it better and probably meet 90% of my needs. However, I quickly realized that this type of thinking was precisely the trap I wanted to avoid.

Yes, I could take on individual responsibilities for specific operations. And, yes I could do this in a way that met my needs better than the inexpensive hosted ASP platforms I was planning to use. However, I was also planning to string together 10 or more ASPs. If I outsourced everything, it might be that each task would be done only 60% as well as I might have liked. However, I would then have a very low cost automated operating system. Most importantly, I would keep my time and energy free to focus on target marketing, which I viewed as the basis of the business's competitive strength. It was entirely possible that if I focused on target marketing to build my customer base, I would develop solutions that could grow the business by quantum leaps—by 300% or more.

Herein lies the tradeoff: Had I chosen instead to undertake

multiple activities myself, they might indeed have been done somewhat better than the existing automated services I could then find. But there would quickly be a multiplier effect. Once I had taken on just a few of these responsibilities, my time would be entirely consumed, and I would be unable to focus on the areas that I believed would allow me to dramatically grow the business. In each area, I might have been able to perform an otherwise automated function 10% to 20% better than an available ASP, with a small associated increase in the size of the business. My conclusion was that it was far better to forfeit these incremental benefits and focus on the areas with the highest potential for dramatic benefits. Once again, the idea of concentrating on the high-leverage points is applicable to building a successful go-it-alone business. I achieved leverage by determining where I could have the highest impact on profits and sales. These were the activities that merited my time and energy. So long as everything else functioned, it was not worth the time or money to make it perfect.

To adopt this philosophy requires far more discipline than one might imagine. There is an enormous temptation to say "That's not quite right, so I will handle it by hand." This impulse must be squelched at all costs. The bias for a go-it-alone entrepreneur must be that all possible activities are automated or otherwise outsourced unless there is absolutely no other choice, which makes it a core activity. Moreover, if you do decide to lock yourself into handling a specific function, you should be asking yourself four additional questions: Have I exhausted every possible source for outsourcing this activity and found that no alternative exists? Is the activity itself crucial? To what extent will it hurt my sales if the business does not include this function at all? Though it may not be possible to outsource this activity today, is it possible to imagine that as the business grows this activity might be quickly outsourced? It's very different to plan an activity that you know you will always need to undertake as opposed to one that you can anticipate automating or outsourcing as the business evolves.

There is something in the human spirit that cries out against the philosophy of the 60% Rule. Few people are comfortable saying "It's good enough, and I need to focus over there." Yet the focus that the 60% Rule can engender is a powerful force. If the basis of your firm's competitive success will exist in one area, it is absolutely essential that you find the time and energy to focus on this area, even if that means that other functions are handled less well.

Are there exceptions to this rule? Yes, of course—primarily with front-office activities. When customers are involved, it's important not to let things slip through the cracks. Good customer service and follow-up are essential for the success of any business. But it may be that a system that is following the 60% Rule will not be as convincing in attracting a small group of customers. This is in essence a failed sales effort, as opposed to poor service for an existing customer. Here, the 60% Rule should apply. It cannot be a priority to spend large amounts of time ensuring that the sales effort targeted at a small group is superb, when the same time could be put into increasing your total profitable sales on a far larger scale.

There are several other aspects to the 60% Rule that are worth noting:

- **The value of just getting your business going is enormously high,** as detailed in Chapter 10. Once you start, you begin to establish crucial learning. If you recognize that no matter what you do at the outset you will probably be substantially changing the business after the first few days, then flexibility becomes more important than perfection.
- **Speed to market is in itself a virtue.** Time becomes a value that overrides perfection. If the priority is speed, then it

trumps fixes that will marginally impact sales. Once again, this idea is admirably brought home by Jason Jennings and Laurence Haughton in the pointed title of the best-selling book *It's Not the Big That Eat the Small . . . It's the Fast That Eat the Slow.*

- **Mass customization will probably eliminate your problems over time.** In Chapter 4, "Do What You Do Best," I described how firms are working toward the integration of one ASP with another and increasingly customizing their ASP offerings. So you can now take this perspective: If you get it up and going today, you can confidently expect that over time, service providers will take you from 60% to 80% of your service goal.

- **Over time, almost any function can become routinized.** As a consequence, many go-it-alone firms are heavy users of part-time workers, such as stay-at-home parents, operating at different locations who handle time-consuming tasks. These workers can typically be located anywhere, with e-mail and Internet services serving as their link to your office.

BUILD FOR FLEXIBILITY

Today's dramatic pace of change in the business world means that in effect, you must plan for a fluid situation in which you can't plan. This is not an oxymoron. In fact, this is good planning!

The way to plan for a dynamic market is to build the business infrastructure, from the start, with tremendous flexibility. This is yet another reason why the ASP model is so powerful as a support structure for entrepreneurs. ASPs are typically based on monthly subscriptions. This gives you extraordinary flexibility to shift the infrastructure of your business as it evolves. If you find that you need an additional support service, it can be quickly and cheaply obtained. At the same time, if you find that one of your existing services is unnecessary, you are not locked into an expensive lease or long-term commitment. A plug-and-play infrastructure is inherently flexible.

There is an additional reason to consistently focus on maintaining flexibility as a core priority: It is possible that though everything is working well one day, a fundamental aspect of the business may have to be reinvented the following day, as the result of a competitor's actions.

MAKE YOUR OWN LUCK

> Chance favors only those minds which are prepared.
>
> —*Louis Pasteur*

Louis Pasteur said that chance favors the prepared individual. Indeed, the more we plan for multiple contingencies, the more likely we are to be "lucky." How often, for example, have you put a spare tire and jack in your car, and then declared yourself to be lucky when a flat tire doesn't destroy a car trip because you can change it immediately? And how often have you failed to take such precautions and declared yourself unlucky when you ended up waiting on the side of the road for hours for assistance?

Luck has unquestionably played a major role in the success of my own venture, Speed Anywhere, but also, I paved the way for luck to head in my direction. Here are two examples:

- Speed Anywhere was originally envisioned and launched as a consumer service. While it was succeeding in this arena, I received a call out of the blue from a business-to-business telecommunications provider who had seen my Internet-based advertising and asked me if I had considered generating referrals for businesses. I responded that I did not know if my marketing techniques would work in selling to businesses rather than consumers. However, I quickly tested my proprietary marketing techniques (the core source of value in the earliest stage of the business) and determined that in fact, they worked even better in a business-to-business context. So I entered that market, and it ultimately became the core of Speed Anywhere's business.

Of course, I have the perspective that I was "lucky" to have received the call from the business-to-business telecommunications provider. Nonetheless, I had also designed Speed Anywhere to be able to take example of precisely this type of opportunity. I had consciously created the capability to test new product offerings very quickly at a very low cost; I had consciously developed a fast, low-cost way of creating new Web sites to offer new products; and I had a system in place for quickly expanding my advertising on Internet search engines to accommodate new offerings. I had missed seeing the superior business-to-business opportunity at the outset of my work, but I was well prepared to take advantage of luck when it visited my doorstep.

It's worth noting here that when I received the inquiring phone call I did not immediately see that the business-to-business market represented a huge opportunity. I was quite skeptical. But I had designed the business with a capability to quickly test and assess ideas, at low cost as they came to me. This allowed me to continuously experiment with new approaches, even when I doubted that the results would be successful. The lesson here? An experimental attitude combined with flexibility is a sure source of increasing the odds of positive luck.

- Later in its development, Speed Anywhere's referral service for businesses seeking a large broadband connection (known as a T1) was called T1 Anywhere (www.T1Anywhere.com), and I envisioned that it had three principle values for the user: First, it provided one-stop shopping convenience. Businesses filled out one short form in less than a minute, and then received customized quotes, based on their specific needs, from those affiliated telecom providers (which numbered over 20) who believed they could meet the customer's needs. Second, T1 Anywhere promised the convenience of fast response. Ultimately, I worked with providers so that the site could promise a response within 12 hours. Finally, I believed that many growing businesses were uncertain how to engage with telecommunications giants. They were not certain that if they phoned the offices of some of the nation's largest providers, they would receive adequate service. The site therefore provided growing businesses with confidence that they were attracting the attention of even the largest providers.

With this mix of values for the user, I envisioned that the site would principally attract growing businesses who wanted to increase the size and speed of their broadband connections. Soon, I found out I was wrong. I discovered that over 50% of the site's users were larger businesses whose contracts for existing T1 services were expiring. In the price-conscious atmosphere that prevailed at the time, these companies were using the site as a quick way to assess available T1 prices and services in the market. The companies knew they wanted to continue using a T1, but they were interested in the availability of lower costs or enhanced variations from alternate providers: They wanted to ensure that they were receiving the best possible value for their spending. Once I recognized that the T1 Anywhere was attracting this customer group, I quickly added specific features to T1 Anywhere that would further enhance its appeal to these larger companies.

Once again, luck played a clear role in my success. I had

not imagined that larger firms, with existing T1 connections, would become a central part of the business's customers. Still, I had consciously built the service with certain specific customer benefits in mind: most notably, fast turnaround, with a wide selection of vendors available through one-stop shopping. What I discovered is that once I created something of value, it attracted a different type of customer than I had expected. I also had the flexibility to quickly increase the attractiveness of the service to this newly recognized customer base.

This second form of luck is common to entities that succeed: They create something that is valuable, and it turns out to be popular with a *different* and *larger group* than they had originally expected. I believe there are two keys to creating this kind of luck: First, build a business that offers real value to meet the needs of your target market, and other specific customer groups may well follow. Second, be in a position to quickly solidify and capitalize on any interest you see from potential customers who are part of a target market that is different from the one you initially expected to attract.

In essence, it is possible to effect how the dice fall. For a new business, luck is what happens when good preparation connects with opportunity.

6
THE MYTHS ABOUT START-UPS

Americans have come to view entrepreneurs as heroes. The image of the modern entrepreneur is our equivalent to the heroic vision, in another age, of the knight in shining armor. By their nature, heroes must be surrounded by myths telling of extraordinary difficulty and courage in overcoming overwhelming odds.

The purpose of this book is not to minimize the achievements of successful start-ups or their founders. Nonetheless, it is important to recognize that many of the tales of the enormous difficulties associated with achieving success are often just myths. By encouraging us to believe that entrepreneurs have scaled superhuman heights, these myths discourage many of us from attempting to realize our own start-up ambitions. These fairy tales have convinced us that people who are unwilling or unable to risk everything they own, to work 90 hours a week for years, to raise millions of dollars in start-up funds, and to immediately hire a large workforce are unlikely to succeed as entrepreneurs. This is just plain wrong.

Here are the central myths about starting your own substantial business:

- It can't exist, because I haven't seen it in the newspapers.
- Extraordinary risk is essential to success.
- The size of the employee parking lot matters.
- Real businesses are funded by venture capital.

MYTH 1: IT CAN'T EXIST, BECAUSE I HAVEN'T SEEN IT IN THE NEWSPAPERS

Discussions of the idea of substantial go-it-alone businesses, established with few employees and limited capital, inevitably raise one persistent question among participants: "If it's now possible to start a business of scale with no money down and few or no employees, how come we don't know about any businesses like this?" This question is absolutely appropriate. As a society, we have become conditioned to believe that the business press is fairly comprehensive in its coverage. If new types of businesses exist in growing numbers, it's natural to assume that the press would be writing about this phenomenon. But this is not a story the press has an interest in covering, and successful entrepreneurs, for competitive reasons, are equally happy to stay out of the media limelight.

Everyone's heard about Andy Warhol's statement that we can each expect 15 minutes of fame. Warhol's comment is generally interpreted to mean that everyone wants to be famous. Today, we could say that everyone except many successful entrepreneurs wants public recognition. One reason most of us are unfamiliar with the formidable successes of solo entrepreneurs is these individuals deliberately avoid the press and all forms of publicity. From the perspective of the majority of these start-up masters, any value publicity creates is far outweighed by the risks it poses: Publicity may bring unwanted competition in their business arena.

During the Internet boom years, the press glorified Internet companies that were focused on offering stock to the public through an IPO (initial public offering). In effect, a symbiotic relationship developed between these firms and the press: Companies that wanted to go public found that publicity played an important role in generating interest in their companies and ultimately their IPO. The press happily obliged in this arrangement by covering these start-ups with intensity. To the world at large, it seemed that these start-ups were the sum total of Internet businesses. In fact, they were not. While widely publicized entrepreneurs were raising money from venture capitalists and attempting to create multibillion-dollar businesses, a second group of entrepreneurs was happily laboring in obscurity. They were taking advantage of many of the new capabilities offered by the Internet, either to create new businesses or to expand their existing brick-and-mortar entities. Because they had no plans to take their businesses public, they were not interested in generating publicity to support the value of their stock offerings. From their perspective, the benefits of publicity were outweighed by the potential that it would lead to new competition. Moreover, the press was, with a few exceptions, only too happy to ignore them. After all, what could be newsworthy about the one-person entities?

I discovered the full extent of this underground "solo success economy" as I traveled across the country as a speaker, author, and entrepreneur. I would frequently meet people who had created hugely successful businesses. Nonetheless, they would talk to me about their businesses only if I swore a blood oath to keep their successes secret. The highly successful, anonymous friend (whose solo business income exceeds $1 million per year) mentioned in Chapter 2, "Principles for Success," is one example. He does not see publicity as a tool to build his business. He has no plans for an IPO. As a consequence, one of his main goals is to stay beneath the radar of potential competitors. He believes that the only result of publicity of any kind would be to invite unwanted competitors into his business arena.

For every rule, there are exceptions; there are certainly many solo entrepreneurs who use publicity as a means of building their businesses. Nonetheless, most go-it-alone entrepreneurs have a far greater aversion to publicity than the typical business. In *Why Smart Executives Fail and What You Can Learn from Their Mistakes*, Sydney Finkelstein, a professor at Dartmouth's Amos Tuck School of Business, confirms that public success invites competition: "Companies that are successful in their marketplace act as an advertisement for others to enter the same arena." Many successful solo entrepreneurs have learned this lesson, and unless they see a compelling business benefit, they actively work to avoid the limelight.

Joe Strahl, the founder of Mr. Trademark, is one example of an entrepreneur who worked to stay under the radar. After several years of my constant badgering, he has finally permitted me, in this book, to discuss his activities in print. Joe was one of the first people to see a practical application of the Internet's inherent tendency to blast apart functions that had previously been handled under one roof.

As detailed earlier, Joe realized that trademark searches involved two distinct functions: (1) searching multiple databases to see if a specific word or phrase (or a similar word or phrase) has already been trademarked and (2) interpreting the results of this search. At the time of Joe's epiphany, lawyers handled both functions and typically charged high fees even when no interpretation of the results was necessary. In a large number of cases, conflicts with earlier trademarks were either very clearly existent or very clearly nonexistent. In general, lawyers needed to become involved in interpreting the results only in the gray areas, when some form of trademark conflict might exist. Joe also realized that the typical lawyer took several days to perform a trademark search, but a specialized business that focused solely on working with these databases could offer a 24-hour turnaround as well as far lower prices.

With these insights, Joe established a low-cost trademark search service that advertised principally through the Internet. Quickly, customers from all over the world started visiting and using Joe's service through the site. Joe's business was a success.

At that point, Joe did not seek publicity. In fact, he did the exact opposite: *He started to focus on how he could prevent potential competitors from becoming aware of his growing success.* One of the things Joe immediately did was to establish a number of different Web sites, under multiple corporate names, that appealed to different types of people: One site, for example, had a very serious, staid corporate image and was called the Trademark & Data Research Company; a second site, called Mr. Trademark, had a friendly, almost counterculture look. He launched other sites, with their own distinct characteristics, as well. Meanwhile, Joe and the exact same trademark search service stood behind all of these sites. This was a smart effort to attract different demographic segments to his business. It was also a brilliant effort to forestall competition. By establishing multiple sites under different names, Joe created the appearance that the trademark search business was already crowded and competitive. In effect, Joe was so concerned about potential competition that he created a smoke screen: He wanted those who looked at the arena to believe that if they tried to enter it, they would be fighting several well-established competitors for customers.

Whenever you wonder why the press hasn't written more about successful go-it-alone entrepreneurs, think of Joe Strahl. Because he is a private company, he isn't required to reveal his profits to anyone. He isn't venture-funded, so he doesn't answer to another entity that might publicize his success. He has gone out of his way to *prevent awareness* of his success.

At the same time, Joe's business is not, on its face, of particular interest to the typical reporter. He is not forthcoming about his activities, his sales volume, or the number of people he employs. Indeed, Joe's business is interesting only in the context of this discussion and the larger trend it represents. It's easy to see why any reporter, bombarded by releases from far larger companies who are planning to go public and are touting their revolutionary activities, would gravitate instead toward writing about aggressive publicity-seekers.

Another reason that some go-it-alone enterprises deliberately avoid any press attention is a desire to project a professional image. Many companies with a limited number of employees can do valuable work for Fortune 1000 companies, but they don't want to appear "small-time" or "unprofessional." One very successful husband-and-wife team that declined to be included in the book expressed this sentiment as follows: "You go to a trade show, make a favorable impression, and then have a professional process for follow-up and sales. The last thing you want is for a Fortune 1000 sales prospect to focus on the fact that you are a husband and wife operating above your garage." Though you may not agree with this concern, it is certainly valid.

Successful go-it-alone entrepreneurs are acutely aware of their competitors. Many of the company owners who did agree to be interviewed for this book adopted strict guidelines in what they would and would not discuss. They were appropriately conscious of the potential for competitors to copy techniques they had developed, and did not want to unwittingly accelerate any transfer of knowledge. As Everette Phillips, the cofounder of China Manufacturing Network and a savvy former corporate executive said, "One of the advantages of being a private company is that we can be private. There are absolute advantages to operating beneath the radar screen, and to keeping our competitors as far from knowledge of our operations as possible."

MYTH 2: EXTRAORDINARY RISK IS ESSENTIAL TO SUCCESS

Scott Adams's popular *Dilbert* comic strip is a good barometer of the underside of business life—the issues, concerns, and craziness of employees in large firms. In one particularly telling strip,

Dilbert asks Dogbert, his semifaithful canine companion, how entrepreneurs are able to live with enormous risks. That's the prevailing view of entrepreneurs: They take extraordinary risks.

Yes, starting a new business involves a certain amount of risk. But so does working for someone else. And the risks associated with being captain of your own fate may be far more manageable and far more acceptable than the risks associated with corporate layoffs and downturns, which are far more likely to be out of your control.

Much of this book is dedicated to demonstrating how go-it-alone entrepreneurs manage and limit the risk associated with their new enterprises. They do this every day in a thousand different ways: gaining actual customer experience with their proposed business concepts before making major commitments to the business, choosing business arenas that have great flexibility in the event they need to shift gears in their quest to succeed, launching low-cost product or service extensions that diminish reliance on a single revenue stream, and so on.

In considering your own venture, don't necessarily assume that the intitiative will involve high risk. Instead, repeatedly ask the question "How can I minimize the risk associated with this new activity?" Once you have acted on every possible mechanism to reduce risks, ask, "Is the risk associated with this proposed venture actually greater than the risks involved in the way I earn my living today?" Unfortunately, many employees are finding that they are already living with considerable, often unrecognized risk. It may be that earning your livelihood by becoming captain of your own well-tested ship is less of a risk.

MYTH 3: THE SIZE OF THE EMPLOYEE PARKING LOT MATTERS

Unfortunately, the notion that successful businesses typically require many employees is a bias that permeates U.S. business culture. Newspaper articles often report the number of employees at a start-up—particularly one that is privately held and does not report its finances—is as an indicator of its credibility. How often have you seen reports such as "the business took off, and in the space of 18 months has grown to 200 employees"?

While writing this book, I thought long and hard about why the number of employees seems to be such a central measure of success. Why is my employee count the first question I am always asked about my business? I think the best explanation is one suggested to me—that this bias goes all the way back to feudal times. In the Middle Ages, the power and wealth of knights was measured by how many serfs worked their land and the size of the armies they commanded. We still hold in awe those who have power over a lot of people. But we have entered an era in which the old measures of success do not always apply. As this book demonstrates, we can envision a new hero: the go-it-alone entrepreneur who succeeds without legions of employees.

MYTH 4: REAL BUSINESSES ARE FUNDED BY VENTURE CAPITAL

In the 1980s, the humor book *Real Men Don't Eat Quiche* was a best-seller. The book played on the stereotype that to be considered a true man, one had to behave in specific ways. Today someone could write *Real Businesses Get Venture Capital*. U.S. business culture grants almost instant credibility to firms that raised millions of dollars in venture financing even when they have yet to produce a product or earn a single dollar in sales. There's always the attitude that you don't have a real start-up if you don't have venture funding. One *Business Week Online* headline read: "Something Ventured, Plenty Gained: Finally, VCs are ready to jump back in—with enough cash to fuel a rebound." The article's message, written when the U.S. economy was in the doldrums, was that the sustained recovery of entrepreneurial activity is possible only with a sustained increase in venture capital investment.

It's time to dump this myth. It is now entirely possible to build a substantial business without raising large amounts of capital first; and to think otherwise is to forgo the very real chance to succeed on your own.

7

WHY YOU DON'T WANT TO BE A FREE AGENT OR A FRANCHISEE

The go-it-alone entrepreneur is neither a free agent nor a franchise owner. This chapter explains why.

THE TRUTH ABOUT FREE AGENTS

> When the music stops, the person with no seat is out.
> —*Rule for the children's game "Musical Chairs"*

What Is a Free Agent?

A great deal has been written about the potential transformation of the workforce into an ever-growing group of free agents. This dynamic is the subject of Daniel Pink's *Free Agent Nation: The Future of Working for Yourself.* But it's essential to distinguish between a go-it-alone entrepreneur and a free agent. In general, a free agent is a skilled individual who makes a living working for others though a series of short- or long-term assignments. The free agent is never a full-time employee and so has far greater freedom than classic corporate employees, in terms of both leisure time and freedom from corporate politics. In theory, a free agent—as compared to a full-time employee—also achieves both greater personal control over his or her own life and a superior income because of the specialized expertise he or she brings to a specific project.

The Unfortunate Reality of a Free Agent Nation

During the dot-com boom, the free-agent lifestyle was widely described and appeared to offer tremendous allure. What was really happening was that we were in an era of real and per-ceived labor shortages, companies were willing to pay for tem-porary workers who happily (and easily) moved from project to project at perpetually understaffed companies.

The end of the dot-com boom dramatically demonstrated the shortcomings of the idea of a large free-agent class. Sud-denly, there was no work for this talented group of individuals. As the job market deteriorated, temporary employees were the first to be cut from payrolls. Free agents, who made a living working for others—with no loyalty to any specific company and none expected in return—had their livelihood viciously ripped away. Free agents are subject to the vicissitudes of the employment market and inevitably experience a boom-and-bust cycle. This is hardly the fantasy of anyone with ongoing finan-cial responsibilities. And it certainly does not suggest a class of people who are likely to have a happy feeling of control over their lives.

The emergence of a free-agent class of workers may unfor-tunately say more about the limited availability of permanent job opportunities than it does about the desire of free agents to live an independent life. As one veteran magazine editor said, "I have never met a freelancer who would not happily take a full-time job." In a March 2004 cover story *Fast Company* magazine expressed an even more negative sentiment, "There is most emphatically a Free Agent Nation today. The thing is, not all of the 9.3 million self-employed asked for citizenship: Downsizing turned many of them into refugees . . . struggling to pay the rent or offering to do the same work for companies they left— for less money and fewer benefits."

The Go-It-Alone Entrepreneur Versus the Free Agent

A go-it-alone entrepreneur is engaged in a quest that is fundamentally different: A free agent is the business, whereas a go-it-alone entrepreneur is working to build a business that exists apart from himself or herself. The advantages of this are multiple:

- **Ownership of a business allows the go-it-alone entrepreneur to capture the full value of his or her ideas.** As a free agent—no matter how well paid you are—if you do something that makes fortunes for your employer or client, you will almost never be compensated according to the full value of what you have created. Temporary workers typically can't negotiate fees based on a percentage of the value they create for the firm. But there's no limit to the rewards available to go-it-alone entrepreneurs. If they understand something unique and execute well, they will reap the full rewards of their efforts.
- **The go-it-alone entrepreneur is building capital.** A successful enterprise is more than a job. It is an asset that can, if the founder chooses, be sold. After a period of time, the entrepreneur has something tangible as the result of his or her efforts. By creating something from nothing, the entrepreneur is far more likely to prosper over the long term.
- **In bad times, the go-it-alone entrepreneur still has a livelihood,** but unemployed free agents largely spend their time looking for work. They are waiting for the phone to ring. They have the will and the energy to work but no place to exercise this drive. It's difficult to think of anything more frustrating. In contrast, a go-it-alone entrepreneur has the opportunity to put his or her nose to the grindstone: The business climate may be difficult, but the entrepreneur has an established infrastructure for earning a living and a place where hard work can still yield positive results.

Fast Company magazine popularized the phrase *free agent nation* and was its biggest booster. But in the March 2004 cover story, "What We Learned in the New Economy," the magazine compared predictions about the "new economy" with the reality. It noted the undesirable lack of job security and low earning power of free agents, contrasting the "Boom Time Buzz" with the "Cold Reality: Free Agent Nation is a jungle." Similarly, a late 2003 *Time* magazine cover story found that free agents "in the trenches often employ a different F word"—*fear,* not *freedom*.

FRANCHISING: A QUESTIONABLE ROUTE TO INDEPENDENCE AND FULFILLMENT

Prospective entrepreneurs frequently consider buying and operating a franchise. But in general, a go-it-alone approach is likely to be more rewarding, and a better use of your time and money, than operating a franchise.

The benefits of purchasing a franchise are well recognized:

- The business model is proven, so the associated risks are generally viewed as lower than when starting a business from scratch.
- By their nature, franchises are repeatable systematized businesses. The most important part of a franchise is the operating manual that details what a franchisee must do.
- Franchisees benefit from the marketing materials that have already been created by the company for local advertising efforts.
- Franchisees benefit from the nationwide advertising efforts and brand recognition of the company.
- Franchisees typically have access to supplies at lower costs because the national operator buys them for all of the franchisees in bulk.

- Franchisors provide valuable training and support structures.

Despite these benefits, I almost never answer a question about purchasing a franchise by saying "Yes, that's a terrific idea." Here's why:

- Franchises are inherently all about following someone else's business ideas and rules. Franchisees lose out on the most valuable element of a go-it-alone business—leveraging their unique talents—though there are rare exeptions.
- The many rules associated with franchises generally mean that franchisees have simply traded one boss for another. The *Wall Street Journal* chronicled the difficulties of one franchisee, in his relations with the franchisor, with the headline "Be Your Own Boss with a Franchise—Not Quite."
- Franchises inherently have little flexibility. Franchisees are betting that a "proven" business will, in today's ultracompetitive world, remain a success. Franchisors typically allow franchisees only limited creativity in building their businesses.
- Franchises, like typical businesses, often require more upfront capital (for the purchase of the franchise license and to get the business started) than ought to be necessary, long hours working at a physical location, and multiple employees. The go-it-alone approach generally turns out to be a far better use of your time, energy, and capital.
- The psychic rewards associated with operating a franchise can be limited. In the article "10 Things Every Franchise Owner Should Know," *Entrepreneur* magazine listed this question first: "How much intellectual stimulation do I need in my work?" The article went on to say that "the vast majority of franchises involve basic retail and service busi-

nesses that require little education or sophistication. After all, if a business is complex and cannot be replicated easily, it probably cannot be franchised. . . . You may well be bored out of your skull after a year or two running a franchised business. How will you handle that?"

These concerns should paint a bold red stop sign subtitled "look hard before you leap." Still, generalizations can be misleading. Despite all the caveats listed above, there may be a franchise opportunity that is both a superb fit with your skills and the equivalent of a go-it-alone business. You might be a Mitch York.

An Exception: Maui Wowi's Franchisee of the Year

Mitch York is one franchisee who succeeded through the go-it-alone approach to business. Before he investigated franchising, he had been a high-ranking magazine company executive and the president of LendingTree (www.LendingTree.com), one of the pioneering Internet-based mortgage services.

York decided that his core competency was in marketing, so he sought a business that would give him the freedom to focus on this skill. He spent several months investigating multiple franchise opportunities and ultimately purchased a Maui Wowi franchise for the New York metropolitan area (www.Maui Wowi.com). The company offers smoothies, coffee and other Hawaiian-themed beverages, and snacks from movable kiosks and fixed locations. Today, York operates multiple kiosks, with hourly part-time employees. After 18 months of operation, York was named franchisee of the year.

York explains that he chose the Maui Wowi franchise precisely because of the creative freedom it gave him: "I liked the concept, but what attracted me was that I could see all kinds of creative ways to apply the ideas that no one had used yet." For

example, York convinced Yankee Stadium to allow him to operate on-site in the 2002 and 2003 seasons and he was the first
Maui Wowi franchisee to operate in a major league baseball stadium. He also realized that there was likely to be a market for
the product at corporate events, which now comprise a substantial portion of his business.

"I looked hard at Sylvan Learning Centers, and I am a great
admirer of the company," said York. "I chose Maui Wowi
instead for two reasons: I did not want to be tied to a particular
retail location. The movable kiosks were attractive. At Sylvan, I
could invest lots of money and then discover that there was a
problem with the location. Second, Maui Wowi was far less
mature, so I could see that there were lots of creative ways I
could add value to the franchise formula." In discussions with
the parent franchisor, York could see that the chain was gen-
uinely open to his innovative ideas. York also noted that the
start-up costs for a Maui Wowi franchise were far below the
much higher franchise fee of Sylvan Learning, and that there
was also the capital-intensive nature of the build-out for a Sylvan location. York also liked the idea of operating without full-
time employees. All of the carts are operated by part-time
employees who work at an hourly rate.

York's description of his focus and operating style sounds
very much like that of a go-it-alone entrepreneur. He is filled
with enthusiasm and knows that he needs to keep reinventing
the business. He says that, "For 2004, the Yankees wanted a
huge marketing fee—I guess every dollar counts when they're
trying to make their payroll. So I decided not to go back to the
stadium. It was an easy decision. I'd already had many other
opportunities that filled the void, even more profitably . . . I will
always need to be developing new ideas for the business to continue to prosper, but that's part of what I enjoy."

York found a franchise that allowed him to outsource all of the things that were not critical to his success—the entire business system represents extreme outsourcing—while he focuses on marketing and business development, his core strengths. This perspective is particularly powerful if we introduce the idea that the Maui Wowi business is relatively simple: It has few moving parts and few management challenges. This allows York to focus his energies, laserlike, on marketing, which determines his ultimate success or failure. In contrast, a Sylvan Learning franchise, for example, would have required that York manage a staff and multiple activities, thereby draining his focus.

The other components necessary for a go-it-alone success are also present: York's ability to serve different locations and different markets creates great flexibility and room for high creativity. And he can leverage his time. He sets up the venue, and then his hourly workers staff it. He gets the maximum bang out of dreaming up new marketing ideas and implementing them.

York's career is unusual in that he has been a successful leader in many distinctly different business arenas, including the classic corporate environment and the dot-com segment. But his experience at Maui Wowi has tapped a particular wellspring of creativity: "Each day I feel a special sense of adventure and energy." There is probably no better way for someone to describe the alignment of his core competency with his individual daily work.

8
MANAGING EXTREME OUTSOURCING

This chapter addresses the central questions associated with using extreme outsourcing to build your go-it-alone business:

- To appropriately leverage what you do best and achieve the necessary focus to create value, how do you decide what should be outsourced and what should be handled in-house?
- Are there specific ways to operate your outsourced efforts so that you realize the greatest possible benefits from this system?
- Are there specific types of business strategies or innovations that are particularly effective when combined with extreme outsourcing?

A NOTE ON GETTING STARTED: EXTREME OUTSOURCING REQUIRES THE ABILITY TO DELEGATE

By definition, employing extreme outsourcing means that you are delegating important parts of your business system to third-party entities. You are giving up control of important parts of your business. The ability to delegate everything except what you do best is an essential attribute for anyone who wants to be a successful go-it-alone entrepreneur.

Avoid the Control Trap

In *The Power of Focus*, the authors discuss the control issue many entrepreneurs confront:

> As a foundation is built, people and systems are put in place to create stability. Gradually the entrepreneur becomes more involved in day-to-day administrative duties. Paperwork increases and what started out as an exciting venture becomes a daily routine, with much more time spent putting out fires, handling people problems, tax challenges, and monthly cash flow.
>
> Does this sound familiar to you? Well, you're not alone . . . this is a very common situation. The dilemma is compounded because many entrepreneurs (and managers) are controllers. They find it difficult to let go . . . Delegation is not their strength . . .

From the beginning, the design of a successful go-it-alone business requires a commitment to an entirely different approach. The business must be established so that you avoid even the smallest essence of the control trap. A go-it-alone business is built on the opposite principle: Success is achieved through focus on a minimal number of high leverage activities, and the outsourcing of everything else.

TRUST AND COORDINATION

As you consider what activities can be outsourced, here is a way of approaching the task: Start with a bias that you want to outsource every possible function that is involved in your anticipated business system. Then, ask yourself these two questions:

- Do you *trust* the third-party business that will be handling the outsourced function?
- Will outsourcing the function make it easier for you to coordinate your overall business system?

If the answer to both of the above questions is yes, then the function should, in all likelihood, be outsourced. Successful outsourcing requires that you believe another business can cost-effectively handle the function as well or better than you. Successful outsourcing should also streamline the operations of your business, and reduce the associated complexity of your responsibilities. The outsourced activity should fit seamlessly into your overall business activities, so that the time associated with coordinating your entire business system is reduced.

DEFINE *OUTSOURCING* BROADLY

Your goal in outsourcing is to create leverage for your efforts: You want to focus your time and energy where it will achieve the highest results—you want to define outsourcing very broadly. Outsourcing can include:

- Relying on an ASP subscription service (such as Salesforce.com) to manage the information associated with sales efforts and prospects
- Engaging someone to work part time (off-site) following your instructions for a repeatable task (such as data entry)
- Engaging a call center to take phone orders
- Contracting with separate firms for everything from manufacturing to the logistics associated with your products (such as warehousing, mailing, and delivery)

Outsourcing encompasses the use of any service operated outside your business that performs a task for you, saves you time, or limits the complexity of what you must do.

It's valuable to recognize the distinction between using an outsourced ASP and using of software or other tools that save you time. You may continue to perform a task, but by using specific tools, you may develop a way of performing that task at far greater speed and efficiency over time. One example might be a software program that helps you to post merchandise on eBay. You have not outsourced the service, but you have certainly increased your own efficiency. In the same way that extreme outsourcing works, the extreme use of productivity-enhancing, easy-to-use software tools can also save you valuable time. Of course, it's easy to waste a fortune on software tools that are "guaranteed to increase your productivity," and you do need to guard against this. The lack of the up-front investment associated with software programs or hardware is also one reason to prefer the ASP model. However, this is one place where it's best not to be penny-wise and pound-foolish. Although cash may be tight, if some specific software, hardware, or service is going to save you several hours a week—and thereby increase your output—you need to realistically ask yourself what that extra focused time is worth for the business. In most cases, you will probably find that the investment is worth it. You'll find that new tools often spark valuable ideas for new opportunities or ways of doing things that you had not previously considered.

THE BRAINS VERSUS THE ARMS AND LEGS

Michael Loeb, the CEO of the Synapse Group, shares the view that "successful businesses have the discipline to focus on one skill . . . and practice that obsessively." To structure a company for extreme outsourcing, he uses the analogy of "the brains versus the arms and legs." You want to keep in-house the critical activities that are "the brains of the operation," he believes. Then, the repeatable, ongoing activities that leverage the work of the brain—the arms and legs—can and should be outsourced.

One way of determining how to decide what activities to outsource involves making a map of the entire process of your business. Begin the map with a list of everything that must happen in your business, from beginning to end. Next, ask yourself, "What are the unique functions that allow this business to create value for the customers and compete in the marketplace? What are the brains of the business that determine whether the revenues and profits of the operation grow?" The activities that do not fit within these criteria should be outsourced.

After you've finished your map and lined up services to handle your outsourcing, you should periodically analyze whether you are on target. While recognizing that everything takes longer than expected, ask yourself how you will be allocating your time for the next 3 months. Do you have contracts to negotiate or specific creative activities to perform? All of these are extremely time consuming. It does not help to be overly optimistic with regard to your efficiency: Try to put together a realistic schedule of how you will be spending your time. If it looks overwhelming, then either you have not outsourced enough functions or you must think harder about how to focus the business to simplify your activities.

Once the business is fully operating, the ongoing administrative maintenance should not take more than an hour a day. This means that work that is neither part of your core competence nor part of your constant effort to reinvent the business should take you no more than an hour each day. You need time and energy for the creative functions that allow you to leverage what you do best, and for building your business for the future.

BUILD IN FEEDBACK LOOPS WITH A FOCUS ON CUSTOMERS

In designing your total business system, keep in mind the critical question of how the system will provide you with constant customer feedback. Successful entrepreneurs are particularly attuned to the needs and responses of their customers, which requires that you be certain to design your business so that this information flows back to you rapidly and without distortions.

All successful entrepreneurs use customer feedback to improve their companies' offerings. Many of them specifically structure their businesses so that they are directly involved in all aspects of customer relationship, even when this might seem—to an outside observer—like a poor use of limited time. Some examples:

- Lars Hundley, the founder of CleanAirGardening.com, handles all the customer service associated with the retail site himself.
- Inder Guglani of Guru.com has been described in the press as adopting "an almost religious reliance on customer feedback." He says, "I cannot believe that companies outsource their customer service functions to other firms. This is a source of essential information. I hope they have the appropriate systems in place for capturing this data."
- Gourmet Gatherings asks customers to fill out detailed evaluations of events.
- Wyck Hay and his wife personally handed samples of KaBoom Beverages to over 20,000 consumers.

Why do they do this? These interactions are often the best source of ideas for improving services and for creating new services. As noted earlier, Mr. Trademark's most successful new offerings consistently arose because customers asked, "Do you do this?" The founder, Joe Strahl, in fact, takes this one step further: "We always succeeded when we expanded [on the basis of] customer requests. Our mistakes typically happened when we expanded [on the basis of] our own ideas of what we thought we could do." These interactions also serve as the best possible radar system for indicating if something is amiss in a firm's operations. Unfortunately, most customers don't tell business owners they are unhappy: They just move their business elsewhere. By doing everything possible to monitor customer satisfaction, these entrepreneurs work to ensure that their customers don't unexpectedly disappear.

PLAN FOR AND EXPECT EVOLUTION

Extreme outsourcing is a constantly evolving process. As businesses grow, new tasks and responsibilities naturally evolve. To allow the time to focus, expanding businesses must continuously look for opportunities to increase leverage by outsourcing additional activities. At the outset of the business, it may not make be feasible to outsource a variety of activities for several reasons.

There may be functions that you don't understand well enough to outsource at the start. You have to experience and work with them before you can create a system that can be followed by others.

At the launch of a business, the volume of a specific activity may also be too small to warrant outsourcing it. However, as the business grows, this situation is likely to change. What's important here is to have a plan from the outset for how and where specific activities will be outsourced once they reach sufficient volume.

In its basic form, the idea of the experience curve, developed by the Boston Consulting Group, provides an added explanation for your ability to outsource an increasing number of functions over time. This idea holds that over time, a company will increase efficiency simply through the act of repetition. The hardest and most time-consuming effort is always the first time you do something. As you do something repeatedly, you develop set ways for consistently performing the same task, and the time required to perform the task decreases. You inevitably create a set system for handling any type of repeatable activities. Once you understand how to perform a task well enough to develop this highly efficient and repeatable system, you can outsource it.

REMEMBER, SIMPLICITY ALWAYS WINS

As you design the proposed infrastructure of your business, remember that simplicity will always outperform complexity.

The go-it-alone businesses typically succeed because of a laserlike focus on solving a specific problem. The founder develops a better way to address the problem, figures out how to create a manageable infrastructure that supports this effort, and remains highly flexible over time. In many cases, this flexibility allows the business to react to market shifts far faster than larger competitors. All of these benefits are heightened when the business is straightforward—and diminish as it becomes more complex.

When Jason Jennings and Laurence Haughton concluded that "It's not the big that eat the small . . . it's the fast that eat the slow," they found that to achieve speed, many companies deliberately worked to keep their business propositions straightforward:

> As we traveled the world in search of the fastest-to-market companies and spent time with their leaders, we heard, "Our business is a simple one," over and over again. At

first we thought we were witnessing humility. Later, we wondered if these accomplished leaders weren't patronizing us and shining us on. Finally, we concluded they were right. Companies that are fastest to market keep their business propositions simple.

In fact, as we conducted further research, we discovered the biggest battle the leaders of fast-to-market companies have to fight is with their own people—those who would complicate the proposition given half the chance.

As a new go-it-alone business, you are by definition the smallest fish in the pond (although I anticipate that you will ultimately outgrow the pond), and can't afford to get caught in a morass of complexity. This doesn't mean that the ASPs you use can't handle complex tasks. In fact, it's their ability to make complexity simple that may make them attractive. The acid test is really whether your business is simple to operate.

Marketing guru Jack Trout makes a similar argument in a book he coauthored with Steve Rivkin, *The Power of Simplicity*:

> Our general education and most management training teach us to deal with every variable, seek out every option, and analyze every angle. This leads to maddening complexity. And the most clever among us produce the most complex proposals and recommendations.
>
> Unfortunately, when you start spinning out all kinds of different solutions, you're on the road to total chaos. . . . Simplicity requires that you narrow the options and return to a single path.

It's a law of nature that focus moves to chaos. Entropy naturally leads ordered businesses to become disordered. There appears to be an equally powerful law of increasing complexity: Things that start as simple ideas and processes can magically transform into overly complex initiatives. Feature creep (the tendency to want to add more choices and more possibilities for customers) is one well-documented example of this. After they have been operating for some time, go-it-alone businesses often attempt to expand into new areas—and they lose focus. Fight that impulse. Start simple and stay simple!

The best test of simplicity versus complexity is probably your intuition. As you go forward, ask yourself how you would instinctively describe your business to someone. If you would say, "It's really very simple. What I do is . . . ," then you're most likely on the right track. Conversely, if your immediate thought is *There are too many moving parts here,* it's critical to stop and reassess your infrastructure.

MONITOR COMPETITORS

It's essential to look at what competitors are doing and try to predict their next moves. As you work to make your product constantly better, you should be studying competitors' offerings regularly. You can bet they are studying yours. Make regular visits to their Web sites, buy their product or service (so long as this is ethical—in most industries, it is just fine), and understand how they are positioning themselves against you, as well as how they are cost-effectively outsourcing functions. You'll have to work at maintaining discipline.

Sherman Eisner, the founder of A&E Home Security, says, "You can't be an ostrich and put your head in the ground." He regularly checks to see what competitors are doing, and he is certain that they are similarly watching him. "I am sure competitors call us—posing as potential customers—to see what services we offer and how we handle customers," he says.

IT WORKS ONLY IF YOU MAINTAIN DISCIPLINE

One of the themes that permeates this book is that running a successful go-it-alone business requires *discipline*. You'll have to work at maintaining the ongoing mix of activities that are required for successful extreme outsourcing. When things are busy, it's far easier to focus on just getting the job done. Unfortunately, that's not enough.

9
LESSONS FROM SOME INVENTIVE COMPANIES

The principal benefits of outsourcing and a bias toward action (getting up and going as quickly as possible) are illustrated in the way some very different firms—TheraSense, the Synapse Group, and eMachines—managed to succeed in highly competitive industries. These inventive companies all achieved success as entities that were larger than what we have classified as go-it-alone enterprises, but when judged against their competitors, they had a remarkably small number of employees and far more limited resources. Both TheraSense and eMachines announced mergers with larger competitors after they had been selected as case studies for this book. I believe this further validates the management success of these companies and makes them even more worthy of close examination.

Case Study: TheraSense Marches in Where Only Giants Tread

For a start-up firm with a new technology, entering a mature industry dominated by giant players is a daunting challenge. This is particularly true in the medical device arena, where established companies such as Johnson & Johnson, Bayer, and Roche Boehringer jealously guard their turf and federal regulations create an additional barrier.

TheraSense developed and marketed a leading-edge blood glucose monitor. The company's technology allows diabetic people to take blood samples from multiple sites on their bodies, including the forearm. Additionally, the test requires only a fraction of the blood required by traditional testing. These two features make the TheraSense monitor essentially pain free.

Today, there are over 16 million diabetic people in the United States who must test their blood sugar at least twice a day. Before the release of the TheraSense monitor, blood samples were drawn from the fingertips, which can be particularly painful because of the concentration of nerves in the area. The TheraSense technology marked a major breakthrough for potentially improving the quality of life of diabetic people.

Despite its technology advantages, TheraSense knew that its launch would be a difficult battle. The company had to manufacture custom glucose monitors, custom strips (which soak up the small amount of blood), lancets (which draw the blood), and lancing devices; acquire specialized packaging; and roll out all of these supplies across the country through both retailers and a variety of direct channels. TheraSense also had to build awareness among doctors and other health care practitioners

To accomplish this formidable undertaking, TheraSense made the decision to outsource all of its key activities but two: the sales force and the manufacturing of the proprietary strip. A variety of different suppliers, including what would become UPS Supply Chain Logistics, were enlisted to handle complex distribution through retail and direct channels, to manufacture the glucose meter, to manufacture the lancing devices as well as the lancets, to provide 24-hour customer service, and to operate the Web site and all e-commerce activities.

Holly Kulp, the company's vice president of professional relations and customer services, explained:

We had limited resources and we wanted to get to market fast. So we decided to focus on our core competency. We needed our own sales force because of the specialized way the product had to be represented to medical professionals. Our core proprietary technology was electrochemically based sensors, and we felt that it was essential that we develop our own understanding of the best way to build manufacturing processes with this technology and that we maintain all of this knowledge as proprietary within the company. We raised almost $50 million for the manufacturing and launch of the product. "That may sound like a lot, but we knew that established competitors in the diabetes market spent that amount on their marketing and sales force alone. To succeed, we had to do things differently."

TheraSense approached its outsourcing much like an army planning an assault. A small team planned all of the critical details, but nothing was finalized until the U.S. Food and Drug Administration granted approval. Then, within the remarkably short period of 90 days, the company was in full swing. Mark Lortz, TheraSense's CEO, and Kulp both note that an important aspect of TheraSense's outsourcing strategy was that the company had knowledgeable in-house experts who could oversee the work of the outsourcing partners. "It was essential that we have people who could set goals, and know how the process should be performing," says Kulp.

TheraSense's launch was a success. The company created an entirely new device category within the diabetes market and established a substantial market share (against large and long-established competitors whom many expected to crush this upstart). Abbott Labs, which wanted to develop a stronger footing in this growing category, subsequently bought TheraSense.

Here are some of the benefits TheraSense achieved through its focus on core competence and outsourcing that are also applicable to go-it-alone businesses:

- **Extreme outsourcing "is what enabled us, as David, to have a sharper spear when we went to fight Goliath," says Lortz.** He guided the company in outsourcing everything possible to ensure that it was handled well but did not deflect the company's attention. Consequently, TheraSense could focus its resources in the high-leverage areas that were critical to its success: building awareness of the benefits of this new kind of product—through its sales force, among health care professionals and the patient population—and successfully developing a facility to manufacture the strips that incorporated its innovative electrochemical sensing technology.

- **The company completed its entire development and roll-out in 2 years, which is half the standard time for its industry.** Outsourcing both saved the firm money and allowed it to get going faster.

- **The company presented a professional image.** "By leveraging world-class resources, we also gave patients and doctors the clear impression that we were here to stay," said Kulp. During its early planning process, TheraSense concluded "that patients had to have the reassurance of feeling that they were dealing with a big company," and that we would fail "if we made people feel that there were compromises involved in doing business with us," she said. "The huge infrastructure of our outsourcing providers" allowed TheraSense to succeed in providing a high level of service and professionalism.

- **Through outsourcing, TheraSense maintained an unprecedented degree of flexibility.** For example, in competing for a major project with one retailer, TheraSense developed and brought to market special packaging within 6 weeks, whereas its larger, established competitor gave up after 6 months because its systems were too inflexible to accommodate this special order.

Case Study: The Importance of Getting Going: The Synapse Group Perspective

Michael Loeb, the CEO of the Synapse Group, is one of the nation's leading direct marketers. At Time Inc., the magazine subsidiary of Time Warner, Loeb helped to guide dramatic growth in *Sports Illustrated*'s readership and later served as the founding circulation director of *Entertainment Weekly*. Then, Loeb went out on his own. Together with Jay Walker, who would later gain fame as the founder of Priceline.com, Loeb cofounded the Synapse Group (originally called NewSub Services) with no outside capital. In December 2001, Loeb essentially returned to Time Warner when the conglomerate's magazine subsidiary agreed to acquire a majority interest (with a buyout option for 100% ownership) in the Synapse Group. The *Wall Street Journal* reported that the transaction valued Synapse in excess of $500 million.

Although Loeb chose to grow the employee base of the company well beyond the size of typical go-it-alone ventures, the company's start-up with no capital and its reliance on extreme outsourcing provide valuable insights for any go-it-alone entrepreneur.

Loeb pioneered the use of credit card billing statements as a vehicle for magazine sales. His business is based on two central insights: First, he figured out how to create value from something that others considered almost valueless. Loeb recognized that credit card billing statements constituted a potentially valuable media that no one had previously used to its best advantage. He also recognized that magazines could be considered a service rather than a product. With a service approach, credit cards statements were a natural vehicle to offer magazine subscriptions that would end when the customer chose to end them, as opposed to the set 1- and 2-year terms created by magazine companies. This approach both put the customer in charge and was more profitable for magazine companies.

What's most important here are Loeb's insights into starting a new venture: "The central rule is to do whatever it takes to get going as fast as possible," he says. Loeb did not negotiate any kind of exclusive deal with credit card companies before launching the business. "Worrying about exclusivity is a high-level problem," he says. These are the kinds of issues that, at the outset, "you don't have the luxury to concern yourself with," he adds. "When you approach a company like Citibank [with whom Loeb made his first deal], you need to make it as easy as possible for them to say yes. I paid them a flat rate so that they knew they would win rain or shine. Whoever was in charge of credit card inserts could say yes, and we did not need to move to high-level executive vice president–type of negotiations, which would probably have doomed the business from the start through delays."

Loeb's decision to offer a flat rate brilliantly secured the future of the business. "If I had offered a percentage of revenues, the credit card companies would have been constantly eyeing the potential profits of the business. Instead, I was assuming the risk, and it would have been a poor use of resources for them to try to recreate our business. In a sense, we became an outsourced revenue source for their previously wasted media. They won, and continue to win, no matter what. Then, how we make money is up to us." In essence, Loeb made it as easy as possible for the banks to say yes and to keep saying yes.

Today, the Synapse Group is the provider of magazine offers on all of the major credit card statements. What's striking is Loeb's success in dominating this distribution channel with no exclusivity agreements. "I am a big believer in getting there first," he says. "Once we established ourselves, we were found money to the credit card companies, and we have a mutually beneficial relationship."

There are multiple lessons in Loeb's experience for go-it-alone entrepreneurs:

- **Get moving.** "Get it off the ground as quickly as possible. If you are first and speedy, you will find ways to ensure you maintain your success," Loeb says. In his view, people spend far too much time putting the cart before the horse. They start negotiating for all kinds of protections and rights before they have proven they can do anything, So, he says, "they never get off the ground."

- **Minimize risk.** Loeb says that "risk is an inherent part of the process, but you work to minimize it as much as possible." For him, this involves "testing absolutely everything you can with real customers so you can understand what works and what doesn't."

- **Don't be afraid of failure.** "Failure is an integral part of the process," Loeb says. "You want to act in areas where's there's lots of margin for error, but you will inevitably see failures. . . . We work hard to encourage action. Errors of commission are inevitable. It's errors of omission that block success."

- **Using extreme outsourcing to get the business off the ground without large investments.** Synapse is still a believer in extreme outsourcing.

Synapse's success is a very real demonstration of the extremely high value of a bias toward action. Once you have a business idea, you want to be as smart as you can do it as well as you can. But the most important thing you can do is begin pushing your idea forward with real customers so that you can start the process of learning and building.

Case Study: Bringing eMachines Back from the Brink

When Wayne Inouye took the helm as CEO of eMachines in March 2001, the company had been delisted from NASDAQ, had just completed a quarter in which it lost $219 million on $684 million in sales, had inventory that was turning over just four times a year, and had poorly regarded products. Most analysts assumed that Inouye would liquidate the company. Instead, eMachines Chairman John Hui took the company private, and Inouye led a turnaround in the notoriously difficult PC market that is nothing short of remarkable.

By the end of 2003, eMachines had been profitable for eight quarters running, achieving a sales volume of $1.2 billion dollars, and had surpassed Gateway to become the number-three desktop PC manufacturer in the United States. While the company is larger than a typical go-it-alone enterprise it had just 139 employees at the close of 2003, which means that the firm was averaging sales per employee in excess of an extraordinary $8.5 million. In 2003, Inouye proclaimed that "other than Dell, we are the only company making money in the PC business." In early 2004, eMachines and Gateway merged, with Inouye becoming CEO of the combined company.

Inouye and his team engineered this extraordinary turnaround by focusing on a few central operating principles:

- **Focus on high-leverage processes.** The company developed a vision of the computer manufacturing and distribution system as a whole. "We looked for the real leverage points that could lead to success, "said Inouye. "Leverage applied to the right places is what leads to success in business today," Inouye added.
- **Use extreme outsourcing.** eMachines followed a path of extreme outsourcing for the manufacturing of products. The company did not view its strength as research and development. Rather, it focused on lowering costs and purchasing components developed by other manufacturers. By the end of 2003, eMachines had what was probably the low-

est selling, general, and administrative overhead costs in the industry at 5.8% of sales, as compared to 8.4% for Dell, 16% for Hewlett-Packard, and 28% for Gateway. Inouye is quick to point out that you can't just outsource and wash your hands of the activity. Although other firms handled the manufacturing, eMachines maintained extensive control and monitoring over the production of its components.

- **Follow the right metrics.** Inouye, the former head of the computer-retailing division of Best Buy Co., saw an opportunity to tie production into the detailed forecasts prepared by retailers, allow retailers to market the product, and optimize this system over time. eMachines began to order PCs from its outsourced manufacturing facilities on the basis of what large retailers, such as Best Buy and Wal-Mart, said they could sell. Under the arrangement, inventory was soon turning over a stunning 70 times per year, and the company does not finish a quarter with a machine unsold. For go-it-alone entrepreneurs, one lesson here is that eMachines developed an innovative process that generated far more effective decision-making returns. With superior metrics, eMachines could reinvent its entire business.

  Moreover, Inouye dramatically lowered the risk in designing new products by collecting detailed data from each retailer on what features were most popular and how much customers would pay for them. This data, which was updated weekly, was used to decide when to introduce new computer models and what features to include. In essence, the company made an unprecedented commitment to a hands-on understanding of customer desires to ensure that it created products customers wanted.

- **Provide a quality experience.** When Inouye joined the company 18% of eMachines's PCs were returned because of defects or customer dissatisfaction. Each return cost the company $200 in devaluation plus shipping. Inouye and his team made a commitment to improved quality and enhanced customer service. By the end of 2003, every customer service call was handled as what the industry terms a "level 3" call, with a technically qualified individual on the receiving end of the call.

eMachines's extraordinary turnaround is a vivid demonstration of a number of the themes explored in this book. The company started by envisioning the business system as a whole and chose to focus on a very few high-leverage points: distribution, demand forecasting, and customer service. Then, it outsourced everything else in order to focus and limit the moving parts in the business, to act quickly, and to keep costs down. And its fanatical attention to customer activity at the retail level—which generated critical metrics—allowed the company to develop a low-cost, low-risk process for launching new products. Finally, eMachines had a clear vision of business model innovation. There was nothing special about the elements that made the product itself. But Inouye conceived a business model that had the advantages of made-to-order manufacturing in combination with retail distribution, allowing the company to offer a quality product at a lower cost.

10

EVALUATING YOUR PROPOSED BUSINESS

It's easy to get caught up in enthusiasm for a specific project. You see a need, you have a workable solution, and your passion is high. But it's vital that you take a dispassionate view of the future. This chapter gives you 11 tests for evaluating your business idea realistically. The best way to use these tests is to consider them as mechanisms for refining your idea.

No business will ever look perfect on paper. What may be most important here is the process: You may decide to go ahead with a business even though it fails several of the 11 tests. But assessing your business against these criteria should give insights into areas in which you need to rethink your business system in order increase your likelihood of success.

THE "ELEVATOR" TEST

Can you tell me how your business will make money in roughly the time it takes for an elevator ride—using a maximum of two short sentences? The Elevator Test is a variation on the widely known elevator sales speech. You need an "elevator business explanation speech." Why? You must be clear on how you will make money. This simple idea may seem self-evident, but in fact many firms start with vague notions of how they will ultimately turn a profit. For a solo entrepreneur, there is only enough time to focus on a few elements, so, the business proposition itself must be simple and straightforward.

Though venture capitalist Michael Moritz works with companies that he anticipates will be far larger than go-it-alone enterprises, he expresses the same viewpoint: a successful start-up must have a laserlike focus on what it hopes to achieve. In 2000, he wrote, in a special issue of *Newsweek*:

> One test we often apply to a new business is the ease with which it can be explained. If someone is able to summarize his company's plan on the back of a business card, it usually means that he will be able to describe its purpose to employees, customers and shareholders. A proposition that takes a paragraph to describe or 10 minutes to explain is dicier. One thing I remember from 1988, when we provided the start-up financing for Cisco Systems, was the stunning clarity with which the company's founders, Sandy Lerner and Len Bozak, were able to explain their business, The entire mission was summed up in three words: "Cisco networks networks.". . . It was a description that has stood the test of time.

THE "THREE RULES MAXIMUM" TEST

One central message of this book is that the success of a go-it-alone enterprise depends on the owner's ability to focus his or her skills in succeeding at a small number of critical areas. As you look at a business idea, you want to ask yourself the following question: *What are the one to three things that are going to determine whether I succeed here?* The obvious follow-up questions are *Do I have the essential expertise to execute well within this focus?* and *If not, can I acquire it?*

THE "YOU ARE THE CUSTOMER" TEST

Put yourself in the place of your prospective customer. Now, ask yourself a series of questions:

- With the range of choices already available to me, would I buy the new product or service this company is offering?
- If so, why?
- As a prospective buyer, am I unique, or are there many people like me?
- Would I buy the product or service *at the full price* that is presently planned?
- How quickly and easily would I buy the service? Would I buy it immediately, or would I require a fair amount of education about this new offering? *Then, stepping back into the entrepreneurial role, ask:* Do the current plans for the business allow for the appropriate amount of time and effort?

From here, you must go on to gather actual market experience with live potential customers.

THE "DIFFERENTIATION AND MARKET HEGEMONY" TEST

Whenever someone says, "This is a huge market and we need to capture only one percent of it to succeed," it's time to turn around and run for the hills. Avoid this trap at all costs! Success demands that your business be distinctive and dominate something. It's far better to be the large fish in a smaller pond than one fish in a giant ocean.

At the height of the dot-com boom, online calendar companies were perceived as valuable. The notion was that lots of people were going to keep their schedules online and that whoever controlled this entry point would have loyal customers. Then the company could charge either for the service itself or for different products and services to these loyal users.

I met an entrepreneur who pitched his new calendar company to me. By my count, there were already six large firms doing what seemed like the same thing. So I asked him, "Why does the world need another calendar company?" He replied that this was a huge market, so there was always room for another player. He described what seemed like minor differences in his service versus others'.

My reaction was that those differences in service were probably not of real value to the typical user—and existing calendar companies would probably add these features anyway. From this perspective, the basis on which he planned to compete against established entrants was (1) either imperceptible to potential users, or (2) he was failing to take account of the likely competitive response to his entry into the market. As a consequence, he was unlikely to compete successfully. With many existing entrants in the market, it is essentially impossible for a company without a highly differentiated product or service to succeed even if the market is huge.

Now, there is a relevant corollary here: If he had said to me, "Yes, there are six existing companies, but none of them serve the market for traveling business women because . . . and this market comprises about ten percent of all the potential users," then I would have been far more intrigued. Here, the entrepreneur would have been segmenting the market and so he could dominate a specific segment. He would have been saying to a specific group of people, "This service is made to meet your specific needs. Here's why it's best for you."

Define your market—even if it is a small segment of a much larger market—so that you have something distinctive that will attract members of that segment and allow you to dominate that arena. Distinctive services win. Me-too entrants fail.

THE "CAN I BE CIRCUMVENTED?" TEST

You may have a valuable insight that allows you to build a substantial business. Then, a supplier or partner will realize that they can replicate your business and eliminate the need for your service or product. Prior to starting the business, you want to assess the risk of this all too common phenomenon and its potential to prevent your long-term success. Businesses can have *structural* attributes that make competition from partners or suppliers unlikely. For example, it would be difficult for an individual mortgage lender or health insurer to create a comparison service such as LendingTree or eHealthInsurance.com, since the basis of these enterprises is the consumer's ability to examine offers from multiple, competing providers. From the outset, you want to consider whether you can structure your business to prevent partners or suppliers from attempting to duplicate the value that you provide to customers.

THE "DOUBLE YOUR COSTS" TEST

Like the elevator speech test, the "Double Your Costs" Test is widely used. It's essentially this: You can predict that things will go wrong, that everything is always more expensive than you anticipate, and that it always takes longer than you anticipate to build a revenue stream. This test looks at how much room you have for error—naturally the more room, the better. Look at your existing plan for profits (your anticipated expense, your anticipated revenues, and the timing of your revenues) and ask yourself the following questions:

- If I double my costs, is this still a good business proposition?
- If revenues are half of what I anticipate for the first year, combined with doubling my costs, is this business still a good idea?

The best business ideas typically leave you a lot of room to make mistakes. And remember, what you end up making money from may not be what you set out to make money from, so leave lots of room for experimentation. This test is probably most valuable when conducted before you put time and energy into test-driving your business. Once you've already perfected your business model—while keeping your day job—you may not have to adopt such drastic assumptions, because you'll have the advantage of real experience to tell you what works.

THE "DEPENDENCY" TEST

A central source of risk in any business can be too great a dependency on one supplier or customer. The rule of thumb is that no single customer should account for more than 35% of a firm's sales. Go-it-alone businesses, which often fit into a chain of activities, are particularly susceptible to a dependency on one company in the chain, so, the questions to ask are these:

- If I look to my left, to my right, above me and below me, is there any firm on whom my business is likely to be particularly dependent?
- If the answer is yes, is there anything I can do to reduce this dependence or to mitigate potential of damage?

One area in which many businesses today are highly dependent is marketing. A few firms—eBay, Google, Microsoft (via MSN), and Yahoo!—control the way hundreds of thousands of people make their living: Search engines and eBay are the primary source of potential customers for many highly targeted businesses. If you are considering a business that is dependent on search engines or eBay, then the relevant question concerns your confidence level that that you will have the skill to reinvent your business if one of these entities dramatically changes its practices, in a way that hurts your business.

If you are considering a business that is heavily dependent on *any* firm, two of the questions to consider are these:

- Will this dependency allow the firm to squeeze my profits?
- What happens if the firm I am relying on goes out of business or chooses to stop doing business with me?

If these risks exist and you decide to go forward with your business, take the time to think through a detailed contingency plan, and formalize it in writing. You may never use it, but by writing it down, you force yourself to really think the issues through and you have it for immediate reference should you ever need it.

THE "CAN IT SURVIVE WITHOUT ME?" TEST

The "Can It Survive Without Me?" Test addresses an upside potential of the business you are considering: Are you building a terrific go-it-alone business that will have the potential to be sold?

It is, of course, terrific if you can create a business that will have a value without you. Remember, this may be only an added benefit. If you create a successful, substantial, go-it-alone business that allows you to pursue your own passions, provides the freedom of being your own boss, and returns a substantial income—all with a minimal capital risk—then you should certainly feel good!

Over time, you will be able to systematize more and more of your business. At some point, it may well be that you have captured all of the specialized knowledge you used—via your core competence—in procedures and systems. At that point, the business can exist without you and has a market value as an independent asset. The appropriate method for determining the value of your business is beyond the scope of this book. One word of caution, however: In our extraordinarily competitive world, the unfortunate reality is that businesses may not have the same value to buyers as they once did. In the past, it was safe to assume that if a business generated a certain return in one year, then (with good management) a similar return was likely the next year. Today, there is the real possibility that without constant reinvention a business will slip dramatically in its returns from one year to the next. A buyer today is purchasing a platform that must be constantly revitalized, instead of a sure thing.

THE "MULTIPLE STREAMS OF INCOME" TEST

One recurring theme in this book is limiting your risk as much as possible. A classic method of limiting risk is diversification. In the context of business income, this refers to the potential of the business to generate revenues from multiple sources. An example of a two-revenue-stream business is the cable television industry. Cable operators derive revenue both from subscribers and from advertisers. The benefits? First, the asset is working harder by generating dollars in multiple ways. Second, if one revenue area declines, the other may not, so the total revenue stream is partially protected through diversification.

The ability to generate multiple streams of income is certainly not a prerequisite for a particular go-it-alone effort to be considered a good opportunity. Rather, it is another factor that adds to a venture's potential value. The classic books on achieving multiple revenue sources are Robert Allen's *Multiple Streams of Income* and *Multiple Streams of Internet Income*.

THE "VULNERABILITY" TEST

The vulnerability test, or "what is the worst-case approach" to analyzing a business opportunity, starts with a few appropriate questions:

- Once I am up and going, what could happen that could essentially kill the business instantly?
- How likely is this possibility?
- How do I anticipate that existing and potential competitors will react to my business?
- Do any competitors have the ability, by responding to my perceived threat, to deliver an immediate knockout blow to my business?
- Why won't existing competitors respond to my market entry?

In some circumstances, you may decide that you have a great idea and that you can execute it well but may feel that as soon as you start, the response from existing competitors will almost certainly destroy your venture. If so, it's probably better to go back to the drawing board.

THE "MORE THAN A ONE-TRICK PONY" TEST

One of the defining characteristics of a go-it-alone business is that its founder has developed quick low-cost ways of expanding the product line. This ability, to cheaply and easily test and launch a new product or service, generally reflects on-the-job experience. But it's still possible, before launching your business, to have some notions of how you may be able to expand your offerings—or not.

You are far more likely to succeed if your business—or the core skills you will be exploiting—will have the flexibility to go in multiple directions. But if you know that you're launching a one-trick pony, stop and think very hard. As a go-it-alone entrepreneur, you have far less room for error.

11

WHEN TO QUIT YOUR DAY JOB

Start-ups backed by venture capital typically require large sums of money to rent office space, hire and pay people, develop the product or service, bring it to market, and slowly achieve profitability. This is a multimillion-dollar activity. In fact, the scale of it is sufficiently high that the original investors in a company almost always know that they are just providing the first round of financing, with additional rounds to follow as the company grows and hopefully makes progress toward its objectives.

In contrast, a go-it-alone business is about investing a limited amount of money in start-up costs (typically from $2,000 to $20,000), generally establishing a home office, and figuring out how the founder is going to live during the period in which he or she builds the business. The risk associated with a go-it-alone business should also be substantially lower: By the time the founder reaches the point of attempting to make the business go, he or she should be well along in developing the product and testing its viability with paying customers.

DID YOU KNOW EINSTEIN DID IT?

In 2000, *Time* magazine named Albert Einstein Person of the Century, because "even now scientists marvel at the daring of general relativity." To Max Born, who was himself a well-known physicist, that "great work of art" [Einstein's general theory of relativity] was "the greatest feat of human thinking about nature, the most amazing combination of philosophical penetration, physical intuition, and mathematical skill." Nonetheless, Einstein worked in the technical area of the Swiss patent office from 1902 to 1909. During this period—working alone, while maintaining his day job—he developed his initial theories and released his first great burst of papers. In 1908, he received an appointment to the University of Bern but kept his patent-office job for another year for security.

Einstein has probably been described as many things. This, however, may be the first time that he is recognized as the model for a go-it-alone entrepreneur. As an individual working alone, he accomplished one of the greatest feats of human achievement while he kept his day job!

DON'T QUIT YOUR DAY JOB UNTIL YOU HAVE NO TIME TO SLEEP

Doing well at your day job while you build your entrepreneurial business is no easy feat. But with determination and hard work, you can do it. The principal benefit of this approach is clear: You can focus on creating the business without the added pressure of racing against the clock to have the business support you. A recurring theme in this book is that you never know what's going to work and it may take two or three separate tries before you hit the right idea. By keeping your day job, you retain the ability to test each of these ideas from the dispassionate viewpoint of someone who doesn't need them to work.

David Drucker, who transitioned from a successful investment adviser to a writer and a speaker on practice management issues, worked at both careers for about 18 months. "I was absolutely certain that my new career would be 400% more rewarding," he says. "But I waited until I was 80% assured that I would generate enough income in the new career to meet my needs."

It's striking how many successful go-it-alone entrepreneurs initially established their businesses by working on them at night and on weekends. Of the many go-it-alone entrepreneurs I interviewed for this book, at least 60% followed this approach. Here are some additional examples:

- David Tartamella, the founder of 1-800-MYLOGO, spent 6 months working at night and weekends to set up his business before he started working on it full time. This was on top of the many years he had spent working on logo design as a personal passion and running an early Web site that displayed his designs to an international group of corresponding individuals.
- Lars Hundley, the founder of CleanAirGardening.com, maintained his day job and continued to work on his MBA while starting his business. He stayed at the job until he "did not have time to sleep anymore, " he says. "It was one of the craziest periods of my life."
- Sherman Eisner founded A&E Home Security Company as a weekend and evening business, while working in a finance-related position for the Treasury Department. Nonetheless, his go-it-alone business is so successful that it enabled Eisner to retire early from his day job with the federal government.

In essence, I am suggesting a tradeoff: Work hard, lose some sleep, get your new business off the ground, and in return you won't put your livelihood at risk.

WHAT DO YOU TELL YOUR BOSS?

Tim Cutting spends his days as an employee at Sun Microsystems and his nights and weekends as the CEO of Niveus Media.

He had already been building his go-it-alone business when he joined Sun, something that he discussed with Sun at the start of his employment. Nonetheless, he said, "When I asked around, [after joining Sun] I found that about seventy-five percent of the people had something going on the side."

Sunny Bates, the president and founder of Sunny Bates Associates, Inc., is a leading executive recruiter and the author of *How to Earn What You're Worth*. Bates, who is widely respected for her views on the future of work, encounters the same phenomenon on a daily basis. "To a person, every executive we interview who is thinking about a career move, or contemplating an opportunity we may have available, is also considering whether to start their own business. I constantly hear about businesses that executives have started on their own time." Her conversations with executives of all ages have also led her to the conclusion that "this is just the beginning. . . . You can't imagine the energy that working executives are now putting into building weekend businesses. I think it reflects a combination of the desire for greater empowerment and concerns about job security."

At one time, it was assumed that workers owed their employers absolute fidelity. In the professional world, if an executive had spare time for thinking about commerce, the expectation was that his or her employer would benefit from it. But we've entered a new era. If companies can lay people off with little warning, then employees at all levels are going to be developing lifeboats that give them greater control over their careers and financial destinies.

However, it is one thing for your office colleagues to know that you have a hobby or side business. It is another to wear it on your sleeve. In discussions at work, consider a side business a part of your private life, which you don't necessarily talk about ceaselessly at the office. If your company has any disclosure policies with regard to outside business activities, you want to be certain to comply with them. *Don't* put your existing job at risk by failing to follow your company's formal disclosure process. Then, it's your life, your spare time, and your business, and there's no need to discuss these activities at the office ever again.

Here's an example of what I mean. I had written a well-regarded article for an industry trade journal about the likely development of advertising on the Internet. At the time, I was general manager of new media at Time Inc., the division of Time Warner that was leading the company's early activities on the Internet. A publisher approached me about turning it into a book—*NetMarketing*. The company had a policy that officially encouraged employees to write books—after all, a good many staff members were journalists—provided that your immediate supervisor did not object and that the company's publishing division, Warner Books, was offered first rights to the book.

Like most busy people, I concluded that there was no way I could do my day job and write a book on the side. As I was considering the issue, I went to see the vice president of communications for Time Inc., Peter Costiglio. After some discussion, he said, "Bruce, you will never have another opportunity like this again. Find a way to do it, even if you have to give up sleeping." He was right. The book became an unexpected best-seller and launched my own go-it-alone business career.

That's why I say that if you have the desire and the determination, find the time. If you have an idea, it represents an opportunity to change your life. Grab it.

The other aspect of this story is how I worked with my division. At the time, I reported to Walter Isaacson, who had written the best-seller *Kissinger: A Biography*, and was at work on his next book, which would be released several years later as the best-seller *Benjamin Franklin: An American Life*. Walter looked at me and said, "You don't have the time to do it," but indicated that he would never stand in my way. He acknowledged that he confronted a similar issue and said that so long as I was doing a good job in the office, finding the time was my concern. I thanked Walter and told him, "You will never hear me discuss it again until the book is released," and that is exactly what happened. I did not discuss any issues related to writing the book, with my colleagues. If I was up late at night, that was my problem, not theirs. How I spent my weekends was my burden. Too often, we have a tendency to consider our private life an open book at work. If your private life includes a go-it-alone enterprise, you don't want to actively keep it a secret, but you shouldn't go out of your way to make it part of your work persona.

Whatever you do in creating a go-it-alone enterprise can also be characterized as making you a more valuable employee. You are perfecting and learning skills that you will undoubtedly use in your day job. In fact, it's important not to undervalue the experiences you are likely to have in getting your own business off the ground, even if you ultimately keep your day job. In *The 5 Patterns of Extraordinary Careers*, James Citrin and Richard Smith discuss the high value of establishing a broad base of successful business experiences. If you're asked about a go-it-alone venture, don't hesitate to talk about a particularly cherished skill you may have acquired through this entrepreneurial effort.

SOME OTHER WAYS OF GETTING GOING

Severance and Savings

If your employer has relocated, closed an office, or eliminated your job, you may well have received a severance. You no longer have a day job to leave, but you do have income for a fixed time. If you have a go-it-alone idea, get busy inventing. There's an increasing trend of people using severance money to meet their income needs while they build a go-it-alone business.

An important point here: If you are the sole source of family income, think hard about how you can stretch out the severance payment. Are there other ways you can make money while you develop your go-it-alone enterprise? Once again, you want to limit your risk and limit the pressure you put on the business to succeed in an unrealistic time frame.

Husband and Wife

A frequent model that I have also encountered is the interplay between husband and wife, in various ways, to start a go-it-alone enterprise. In many cases one spouse may continue working, and though it pinches the family income, it's sufficient—for a time—to allow the other spouse to get his or her business up and going. An example would be Krisan Marotta, who started her business, Krisan's BackOffice, after she had been an at-home mom. Her husband supported the family while she got the business going. Later, she supported the family while he started his own entirely separate business.

Working on your new enterprise at night and on weekends, while you keep your day job, isn't always possible. One entrepreneur who had to leave his existing employer—because of potential conflicts—before starting his new career is Chris Palermo. Today, Palermo's enterprise, Global Communication Networks, Inc. (www.gcnsolutions.com), is a substantial success and one of Sprint's top five revenue producers in the nation.

Palermo had a skill in selling and customer service, with experience as a global account manager at AT&T, and a district sales manager at Cable & Wireless. He saw the opportunity to develop a telecommunications agency in his home turf of South Florida because he believed that business customers were frustrated by the lack of good customer service, which he knew he could provide.

His approach to creating the business reflects a discipline that's important for any go-it-alone initiative. He says:

First, my wife was working and I had one substantial commission payment that I would still receive from my previous employer. My wife and I figured out our finances and determined that we could live for a year on her income and this final payment. We were very serious. I had a year to make it work or I was honor-bound to go back to a job in the corporate world.

To start out, I worked every day with extraordinary discipline. I used what's called the fifty-point system. Each day, you have to earn fifty points. A successful phone contact with someone at a business with whom you have never had any previous contact counts as one point. An appointment to meet with someone counts as ten points. Your day does not end until you have hit fifty points. It's really sales 101, but as people progress, they forget the need for discipline, focus, and determination. I really think a major reason I succeeded was that I stuck to this very disciplined approach to generating new customers, and because it was my all-consuming focus.

In this era of consolidation of major music labels, Bob Hauver and his wife, Patti DeMar Hauver, decided that there was an opportunity to build a niche record label, for which they would both perform and sign other acts. As a result, Hudson Valley Records (www.HudsonValleyRecords.com) was born. Bob kept his office job during the week, while Patti worked from their home on marketing the label. The firm has not yet reached the point where it can support the family, but the Hauvers are very happy. "We have had somewhat less income than we might have if Patti had taken a regular job," said Bob. "And it's not clear that this will ever be a real financial success. But it has absolutely been worth it. We formed a band and cut and distributed our own records as well as those of other worthwhile artists. It's been hard work but incredibly exciting. We are doing something we have always wanted to do," he said. Hauver has now retired. He notes, however, that while maintaining his day job, he treated Hudson Valley Records as part of his family life—not a secret, but not part of his work persona either. "The two worlds just did not intersect," he says.

Seniors

Increasingly, seniors who have retired from one career are looking to keep working. A go-it-alone business is, in many ways, an ideal option. To start a business of this type, typically requires someone with time but not necessarily capital. This matches the situation of most seniors who are looking to continue working: Many want to supplement their incomes but don't want to invest their savings in a new business endeavor, and many have the time to build the business without the need for immediate financial returns.

In addition, go-it-alone businesses can in many situations be run from anywhere and can be structured specifically as part-time efforts. People looking for part-time work, or work with flexible hours, or even work that allows them to travel frequently should be able to find it here.

12

THE RACE TO LIQUIDITY: WHY VENTURE CAPITAL IS NOT FOR YOU

THE AMERICAN OBSESSION WITH VENTURE CAPITAL

One of the unfortunate aftereffects of the dot-com boom has been that by and large, the business community now equates business start-ups with venture capital investment. As noted earlier, this has led to the myth that the only "real" start-ups are funded by venture capital. In fact, venture capitalists themselves are quick to point out that they support only very specific types of investments, and that the vast majority of start-ups are and should be financed through alternative methods. This chapter explains why a go-it-alone business and a business funded by venture capital are, in essence, at opposite ends of the spectrum of entrepreneurial activity.

THE PRIORITIES OF A VENTURE CAPITAL FIRM

Since the mid-1980s, Stewart Alsop has been one of the nation's most respected technology industry commentators and participants. Among his many roles in the industry, Alsop served as editor in chief of *InfoWorld*. After joining the venture capital firm of New Enterprise Associates, where he was a general partner, he continued for several years to provide insightful commentary through a regular column in *Fortune* magazine. In a detailed interview for this book, Alsop provided a candid view of how the venture capital industry works.

Alsop believes that venture capital activities can be reduced to two very simple notions: First, a venture capital firm is a money management firm. Venture capital firms raise large sums of money from limited partners who are typically institutional investors, and are expected to provide a high return on this money. "You hear venture capital partners talk about being in the business of technology: They are not. They are in the business of managing money," he says. In essence, think about venture capital partners as rational investors who are seeking the highest possible return for their clients.

Second, the typical venture fund has a life of 10 years. This means that the firms expect to distribute all of the proceeds of the funds back to the limited partners within this period. While that may sound like a long time, it can take several years to invest the money received in a single fund. The central point here is that the typical venture capital investment needs to achieve liquidity anywhere between 3 and 6 years, and this need for liquidity becomes the driving force behind any venture-funded investment.

Once an entrepreneur accepts venture capital investments, he or she is inevitably setting the company on a specific course. The firm must drive as rapidly as possible toward a liquidity event, which means either an IPO, in which the firm's stock is offered for sale to the general public, or the sale of the entire firm to a larger company. This liquidity event is what allows the venture firm to return earnings to the limited partners who have invested with it.

This drive for rapid liquidity also means that the firm needs to grow very fast and become valuable very fast. Neil Weintraut, now a partner at Palo Alto Venture Partners, is also a well-known Silicon Valley veteran. In a detailed article in *Fast Company* magazine several years ago, Weintraut emphasized the need for fast growth even more strongly than Alsop. The story said:

To build a fast start-up, says Weintraut, you need to hire fast people. More important than time to market, he says, is "time to hire," since the latter will determine the former. "An entrepreneur has only one job: to hire," Weintraut explains. "Starting a company is no longer about raising capital; it's about raising teams." The single biggest challenge for any start-up is finding people who will enable you to move fast.

The fast liquidity needs of venture capitalists also means that, in general, they limit their investments to a few sectors where businesses grow rapidly: semiconductors, health care, telecommunications, pharmaceuticals, technology, media, and software.

TWO VERY DIFFERENT PATHS

The above discussion demonstrates the dramatic differences between the incentives of venture-funded companies and go-it-alone initiatives. Venture capital funding is necessarily about managing fast growth with many employees, founders sharing control with investors, and rapidly achieving a liquidity event through a sale of the firm or an IPO. In contrast, go-it-alone initiatives are oriented toward profitable cash flow, growth that is merited by the cash coming in, founders retaining control, limited management, and a focus on a a limited number of employees doing what they do best.

The type of business you have will generally dictate the funding strategy. If you envision a business that will rely on large amounts of capital to get off the ground, then you probably need to raise venture capital. Alternatively, if you are in an industry that is not popular among venture capital investors, you are unlikely to have the real option of seeking this type of funding. Venture investors are also unlikely to back a firm that does not want to grow its employee base. Don't spend time courting venture capital investors (1) if you don't want to grow fast, (2) if you don't want to manage lots of people, (3) if you don't want to share control of the business with investors. If you envision a business that is not in the high-tech, media, or health care arenas, recognize that your chances of attracting venture capital are remote. In these situations, you may want to consider the very viable go-it-alone route to success.

13

MISTAKES HAPPEN—LEARN FROM THEM

The things which hurt, instruct.

—*Benjamin Franklin*

THE IMPORTANCE OF LEARNING

The value of focus is stressed throughout this book. But there's one aspect of it that hasn't been discussed: Focus is important so that you can learn as much as you can as fast as you can. Without a dedicated concentration on learning, your chances of long-term success are slim.

As a solo entrepreneur, you are going to try things. Some of these will work; others will not. What's most important, however, is that you have the ability to learn from what you are doing and thereby continue on your path to success. In *Failing Forward: How to Make the Most of Your Mistakes*, John Maxwell quotes William Dean Singleton, the co-owner of Media News Group:

> Too many people, when they make a mistake, just keep stubbornly plowing ahead and end up repeating the same mistakes. I believe in the motto, "Try and try again." But the way I read it, it says, "Try, then stop and think. Then try again."

This is the ideal of the experimental attitude, which is also emphasized throughout this book. Building a business today is a never-ending process of trying something, learning, and trying more—on the basis of what you have learned. Within this context, *mistake* is just another word for something you have learned not to do again. In the corporate world, a mistake may be a cardinal sin. At minimum, you probably have to convince someone above you in the corporate hierarchy that despite the mistake, your performance is still terrific. When you are a solo entrepreneur, that kind of thinking is irrelevant. In fact, the reverse is true: You must make mistakes because they are an inevitable part of the process of learning what works.

The key to making "good" mistakes is to limit your downside risk. You want to experiment, and then experiment some more, so that your mistakes have consequences that are as limited as possible.

WHY BUSINESSES FAIL—THE WARNING SIGNS

Sydney Finkelstein's *Why Smart Executives Fail and What You Can Learn From Their Mistakes* focused principally on large firms, but many of Finkelstein's findings are applicable to go-it-alone businesses as well. One particularly useful aspect of Finkelstein's work is his indicators, or warning signs, that there may be trouble on the horizon. These are the most relevant warning signs for solo entrepreneurs:

Complexity

In Chapter 8, this book argues that simplicity is a critical component for go-it-alone success. Finkelstein similarly finds that "unnecessary complexity is a warning sign because it tends to create bigger problems than it solves." As a consequence, you should be concerned if the business is starting to seem overly complex or if the solutions to a specific problem seem complex.

Success Leading to Complacency

"One of the best generic warning signs is . . . success," Finkelstein writes. He lists a host of reasons why successful companies can quickly fail, including these:

- When things are going well, companies often don't stop to understand the true reasons for their success, so they don't see that things need adjustment until it's too late.
- Companies that are "successful in their marketplace act as an advertisement for others to enter the arena." A publicly recognized success can breed more intense competition.
- It's easy "to let your guard down when you are awash in success. It's only natural." Finkelstein quotes Machiavelli, who aptly said, "There is a common failing of mankind never to anticipate a storm when the sea is calm."

In his influential book, *Only the Paranoid Survive: How to Exploit the Crisis Points that Challenge Every Company*, Andy Grove, the former Chairman of Intel, issues a similar warning. "Complacency often afflicts precisely those who have been the most successful. It is often found in companies that have honed the sort of skills that are perfect for their environment. But when the environment changes, these companies may be the slowest to respond properly."

For go-it-alone entrepreneurs, these injections reinforce two central operating principles discussed repeatedly in this book: the need to constantly reinvent the business and the need to understand the real reasons that the business creates value. Finkelstein's findings do, however, add an extra urgency to these principles: Entrepreneurs must be reinventing their businesses even when everything looks terrific. Once you wait for competition to emerge or for problems to become crystal clear, maintaining your earlier success will be far harder than if you assume that competition will be coming and act accordingly from the beginning. You must always be looking over your shoulder.

Not Recognizing, Acknowledging, and Correcting Mistakes

Mistakes are an inherent part of business life, says Finkelstein: "When it comes right down to it, you can't afford not to take risks. Calculated risks are essential to business. And, by definition, when there are risks, there are mistakes." However, what distinguishes companies that succeed from those that fail is their ultimate ability to recognize that a serious mistake is happening and to change direction before the ship goes down.

Finkelstein writes that serious mistakes "tend to evolve, meaning there really is an opportunity for executives to step in before it's too late and take action to disrupt the pattern and avoid ultimate failure." For large companies, he advocates a series of solutions that include "a culture of openness"; establishing "multiple avenues of debate, discussion, and data" so that people have a voice; and creating a learning organization that is open both to new information and to shifts in direction.

Recognizing when the business may be caught in a serious mistake is equally critical for a go-it-alone business. The specific solutions, however, must be somewhat different. Finkelstein's focus on openness and learning are undoubtedly correct, but what does that mean for a go-it-alone business? It means doing everything you can to constantly validate your assumptions—talk with customers as much as possible, monitor competitors and marketplace responses to their initiatives, and establish metrics that are likely to serve as early warning signals of vital marketplace changes. The almost fanatical customer-centric attitude demonstrated by many of the go-it-alone businesses discussed here is good model for this kind of focus. If customers are thinking about doing anything different that will impact your business, you must recognize this change, and act on it, as early as possible.

It also means that you need to take time out to regularly engage in an exercise of what if. Make a list of the things that could seriously undermine your business, from the possible collapse of a central client business, to the loss of an important marketing channel. Paste the list on the wall in your office. Look at it regularly and ask yourself, *How do I know these things are not happening? What if this assumption or that assumption is wrong? Is there something else I could be doing to test this understanding?* There is one very important distinction between a go-it-alone enterprise and other businesses: Only you can ask yourself the hard questions. There is no one to do it for you, and you ignore them at your peril.

THE NEED TO FOCUS ON MAINTAINING FOCUS

A Frequent Mistake: Attempting to Expand from Focused to Comprehensive Services

One phenomenon that seems to repeat time and time again is the unsuccessful attempt by go-it-alone entrepreneurs with a highly focused service to make the giant leap to providing a comprehensive service. When you expand your offerings, you want to understand—as clearly as possible—the similarities and differences between what has made you successful and what you are considering. You must be particularly cautious about anything that hinders your laserlike focus on your successful offerings. Typically, success in offering a number of related, highly focused services does not translate into success into offering a comprehensive suite of services in this same general area.

Recognize that over time, there is a natural tendency toward drift. In *Focus: The Future of Your Company Depends on It*, Al Ries eloquently describes how easy it is to move from focus to company-killing branching out. "A successful company usually starts out highly focused on an individual product, service or market. . . . But success creates something else: the opportunity to branch out in many directions," he says. As a result, "over time, the company becomes unfocused. It offers too many products and services for too many markets at too many price levels. It loses its sense of direction." In *The 80/20 Principle*, Richard Koch expresses this same idea in a different way: "Where a business is dominant in its narrowly defined niche, it is likely to make several times the returns earned in niches [where it faces other strong competitors]. . . . Simple is beautiful."

Fight the natural tendency toward drift. In *Who Says Elephants Can't Dance?* Lou Gerstner calls the "grass is greener" mentality "the most pernicious" reason companies lose their focus and ultimately fail. It's easy to become enamored of a new idea but far harder to continue the heavy lifting needed when you encounter a problem in your core business. It's the companies that stay the course and work through these problems that succeed. As Gerstner writes, "Stick to your knitting. . . . History shows that truly great and successful companies go through constant and sometimes difficult self-renewal of the base business. They don't jump into new pools where they have no sense of the depth or temperature of the water."

But it's important to distinguish between diversification that maintains focus and diversification that is defocusing. As noted before, successful go-it-alone businesses are good at inexpensively testing new offerings and rapidly bringing them to market. These offerings are part of a laserlike strategy: They enhance the core business, they rely on the same repeatable functions, and they require very little extra infrastructure. In essence, they are part of the same basic focus.

One simple test for distinguishing between valuable diversification and diversification that diminishes focus is the amount of new infrastructure required for a new offering. By and large, if no new infrastructure is required, then you are enhancing your business and maintaining your focus. If new infrastructure is required, you should think seriously about whether this new initiative will quickly lead to weaker business by increasing complexity.

14

SUDDENLY, JUST ME

In *The Elephant and the Flea*, British social philosopher and business commentator Charles Handy describes his decision to go out on his own. He notes that after deciding "I shall just be Charles Handy . . . it took me some time to be proud of the fact that at conferences and the like I had no institutional affiliation attached to my name. It felt naked." Handy had spent 10 years working at the Royal Dutch/Shell Group and then 4 years as the prestigious Warden of St. George's Houses, a conference and study center located in Windsor Castle. He eloquently describes the sudden, jarring experience associated with going-it-alone: "The problem comes . . . when you have to define yourself without the corporate prop. We had many friends when we lived and worked in Windsor Castle and many invitations to glamorous social events, invitations that mysteriously evaporated after we left."

The sudden adjustment from working in a large corporation to operating a solo start-up can be wrenching. Here are some guidelines if, in fact, you are contemplating or are already amid this transition:

- **Know that nothing happens unless you make it happen.** In an established entity, things happen. You have responsibilities. But when you begin a go-it-alone initiative, an infrastructure with resulting activities exists only after you have created it.

- **It's essential to recognize that there is no A for effort.** As the comic strip *Dilbert* constantly reminds us, people advance in the corporate world for a variety of reasons, many of which may be unrelated to actual performance. To their credit, some companies even reward employees for daring to undertake an innovative initiative that fails. (In these cases, they are wisely betting on the value of the experience and learning that the employee gained during this process.)

The start-up world is, in this regard, far more absolute and far more Darwinian. This book repeatedly discusses methods for mitigating risk. But after you've built in as much protection as possible, whatever risk remains is something that you must own completely. In corporate life, it may be acceptable to say, "My sales did not meet quota because my largest account went bankrupt." In a go-it-alone endeavor, you can succeed only by taking responsibility for dependence on a large account that went bankrupt. The exciting part of the effort is that you can capture the full rewards of everything that happens to you. The downside is that you must take responsibility for everything that happens to you.

In *Failing Forward*, John Maxwell amplifies this idea. Maxwell's theme is that failures are inevitable and that what distinguishes achievers from everyone else is their attitude toward failures and their ability to learn from them. He writes: "The only way to exit the failure freeway and see the new territory of achievement is to take full responsibility for yourself and your mistakes. . . . Take a hard look at a very recent failure that you have considered not to be your fault. Look for anything negative in the failure that you should claim responsibility for. Then own it."

When you go-it-alone, you must make the jump from blame to responsibility. When problems occur in your business (and they assuredly will), it ultimately does not matter why they happened. You must to take responsibility for them to make the business succeed.

In *No Excuse Leadership: Lessons from the U.S. Army's Elite Rangers*, Brace Barber echoes a similar theme. The rangers are taught that they must succeed and therefore must take responsibility for every outcome, even if there is an appropriate reason for failure. Barner writes: "The first time you stop yourself from giving a perfectly legitimate reason why the job did not get done will be tough; do it, and then do it again. You will see yourself start to succeed beyond your peers who allow themselves reasons to fail. . . . Imagine the effect a philosophy of 'No Excuse' will have on your life."

- **Be prepared to sell.** As a go-it-alone entrepreneur, you must be ready to convince people that your initiative has merit. This may take the form of what is considered classic selling: convincing people to buy your product. Even if you do not see yourself involved in classic selling, you will still, in all likelihood, need to be a persuasive salesperson: You will most likely need to convince entities to do business with you—either as a provider or as a recipient of your work.

Mark Lortz, the CEO of TheraSense, reinforces this point in describing the company's successful outsourcing initiative. "We needed to convince large, world-class providers like UPS that our business would become significant, and that they were getting in on the ground floor. Our size as a start-up was not interesting to them. UPS had to believe in our growth potential." TheraSense's ability to enroll other entities in its vision of success was part of what made the company a success.

The importance of your ability to be persuasive cannot be underestimated. There are endless stories of entrepreneurs who have a bold vision but fail because they can't enlist the participation of other entities that are critical to the success of their venture. This point is also demonstrated in the story of Synapse's growth: For Michael Loeb, a critical factor in getting the business off the ground was convincing the large credit card companies to work with his firm.

- **Be prepared to demonstrate credibility.** When you call a large firm while working at another large firm, the dynamics are fairly clear. Both entities may have a vested interest in working with each other. As a consequence, your call is likely to be returned without too great a delay and your credibility is not in doubt. When a go-it-alone firm calls a large firm, the dynamics are very different. Imagine you are an employee at a large company. Now, how would you react if someone called you with a proposition from a solo entity? What would compel you to take or return the call? How could a solo entrepreneur demonstrate sufficient credibility so that you would consider doing business with this one-person enterprise?

  A confident attitude will go a long way toward demonstrating credibility. It is absolutely essential that you project confidence in your ability to handle whatever task you are discussing with a potential customer, client, or supplier. As a go-it-alone entity, you are effectively asking people to trust you. How can people have confidence that you will deliver on your promises if you appear to doubt yourself?

- **Be absolutely focused on getting paid.** At large corporations, getting paid is not a central focus for operating personnel. Typically, separate credit and billing departments handle all of the issues associated with payments. When you run your own firm, cash flow becomes a central concern and the timely payment of bills becomes essential. The best approaches to ensuring you are paid on time by both large and small companies is beyond the scope of this book. It is, however, a topic that is addressed in many guides to starting a business. As you get started, it's critical that you focus on this issue.

- **Think through your own support system and the extent of your need to stay connected to other people.** Although you have chosen to go-it-alone, you will benefit enormously from substantial connections to other people, both peers and mentors. You will need ongoing connections to balance what may be a life of greater solitude than your former existence, and at certain moments all of us need people with whom we can share—and dissect—ideas. Even the simple act of describing your business or activities to someone may, in itself, help you to clarify your own thinking.

- **Never be afraid to ask others for help.** Many of us hesitate to ask for assistance, but don't. There is no shame, loss of honor, or disgrace in asking for a favor. Fundamentally, people like to help other people. And when someone assists you, it can help to cement an ongoing relationship. People who have helped an individual often start to take a proprietary interest in seeing that person succeed. But do make it as easy as possible for people to assist you: Always be specific whenever you ask for aid.

   Indeed, in his autobiography, Ben Franklin, who was one of the most successful entrepreneurs of his age, makes special note of this aspect of human nature, which remains true today. Franklin cites what he calls "the truth of an old maxim I had learned, which says; 'He that has once done you a kindness will be more ready to do you another than he whom you yourself have obliged.'" Franklin recognized that once someone has done something to help you, they are now in the habit of helping you and invested in your ongoing success.

CONCLUSION

Fear Is the Enemy

> You gain strength, courage, and confidence by every experience in which you really stop to look fear in the face. . . . You must do the thing which you think you cannot do.
>
> —*Eleanor Roosevelt*

There is one final roadblock that for many people is the most significant barrier to pursuing an entrepreneurial venture: fear. But you can't let fear run your life.

The idea that fear prevents many of us from pursuing our entrepreneurial dreams is not new. Most of us are familiar with Dale Carnegie as the sales guru who authored the classic book *How to Win Friends and Influence People*. What most of us don't know is that in 1944, Carnegie wrote *How to Stop Worrying and Start Living*, which has sold over six million copies. A central theme of the book, still relevant today, is "how to break the worry habit," which keeps people from realizing their goals.

I sought approaches to overcoming this obstacle. My research led me to several very different perspectives, each valid. Take what you need here to overcome your fear and start up the go-it-alone business that matches your aspirations.

DR. KATHLEEN HALL: UNLEASH YOUR INHERENT CREATIVE ENERGY

One of these perspectives comes from Dr. Kathleen Hall, the author of *Alter Your Life*. Dr. Hall is a renaissance woman: A successful entrepreneur in her own right, she writes and speaks widely on the results of her studies of meaning and work. In her book, she discusses how our daily lives can be awakened with meaning and purpose.

Dr. Hall notes that we should start any discussion of fear by recognizing that fear is healthy. If we are afraid, it is a sign that our intuition is telling us to look hard at something. We can turn fear from a negative into a positive by using it to help guide us to areas of our enterprises or associated lives that need to be addressed. But fear becomes unhealthy when it is manifested physically or becomes a driving force in our lives.

She believes that the pursuit of your passion releases energy. "When you are doing what you should be doing, you know it, and your body knows it," she says. She describes the resulting feeling of individual power, of control over your life, and the associated release of extraordinary energy that accompany these activities. It is the release of this burst of positive energy, she says, that gives you the strength to get past fear.

In *Tiger Heart, Tiger Mind: How to Empower Your Dream*, Ron Rubin and Stuart Avery Gold express a similar idea:

Instead of dwelling on your self-doubts, picturing the menace that waits, visualize your dream, focus on the specific image of the desire you seek. Passionately believe in the probability of succeeding in turning your dream into a reality. Passion empowers. The more passionate you are about living your dream, the more you will begin to assert control over your fear. And while you may never rid yourself of having fear as a constant companion, you can learn to take charge. . . .

From the perspective of this book, these ideas can perhaps be summarized as follows: You can overcome fear by pursuing your passion and doing what you do best. Once you start this pursuit, the resulting energy will be so strong that it will overwhelm your destructive fears.

Dr. Hall also suggests that when confronted with a life-changing choice, you use guided imagery. The scenario she uses for herself involves imagining herself near the end of her life, with a grandchild asking what she most regrets and what she is most proud of. To her, the ability to say to her grandchild "I did it—I wanted to and so I tried" is often more valuable even than saying "I succeeded." Using your imagination to find out what you really want out of life will create in you the determination to get past fear.

JOE GIRARD: CONFIDENCE BREEDS CONFIDENCE

Joe Girard, who has been described by the *Guinness Book of World Records* as the world's greatest salesman, details the start of his incredible career in *How to Sell Yourself*. Girard describes listening to a sermon by Dr. Norman Vincent Peale, in which he said that the most powerful word in the English language is *faith*, but that there is a second word "so powerful that if you let it, it can wipe out faith." Girard continues:

> "That word," [Peale] said, in tones that showed his contempt for it, "is a four-letter word called fear." Again, he spelled it. "Fear that you can't be or do something, fear of the past and its consequences, fear of tomorrow for what tomorrow might bring, fear that you might fail."

Girard tells how Peale's vivid description perfectly described his early career. Prior to age 35, "fear became the ruling factor in my life." He describes his own climb out from under this destructive weight and concludes that there are "five rules to

help banish fear and replace it with self-confidence and
courage."

1. Believe in yourself. . . . You can if you think you can.
2. Associate with confident people. Stay away from negative,
   fearful people. . . . Confidence breeds confidence.
3. Tune up your confidence machine. (Develop confidence in
   yourself.)
4. Be the master of your ship. . . . Henry Ford said that all confident people gained their courage by facing their fears
   instead of running away from them.
5. Keep busy. In a busy person fear and self-doubt have little
   time to dwell.

In essence, Girard holds that the busy person who *expects* to
succeed taps into a self-reinforcing, virtuous circle: Each day, as
the reality of success unfolds, the individual's daily activities
build ever greater confidence and dispel fear.

DR. SUSAN JEFFERS: FEEL THE FEAR AND DO IT ANYWAY

Dr. Susan Jeffers, a noted psychologist, is the author of multiple
books, including the best-selling *Feel the Fear and Do It Anyway*.
In her writings, Jeffers suggests that our fears stem from self-
doubt, a lack of confidence that we will be able to handle the
situations that confront us. In *Feel the Fear and Do It Anyway*,
she asks, "If you knew that you could handle anything that
came your way, what would you have to fear?" In essence, Jeffers holds that the greater our self-confidence and the greater
our belief that no matter what happens "I'll handle it," the more
our fears diminish. Jeffers writes, "Never let these three words
out of your mind—possibly the most important three little
words you'll ever hear: I'LL HANDLE IT!"

MOVING BEYOND FEAR

Hall (a spiritual thinker), Girard (a great salesman), and Jeffers (a psychologist) approach the problem of fear from very different backgrounds, but their conclusions are remarkably similar. They all recognize that fear is a destructive impediment to an independent business career, and they all recognize that action dispels fear. So start your go-it-alone business despite your fears—and then feel the resulting energy and self-confidence, keep fear away.

A FINAL NOTE

> Whom the gods wish to destroy, they give unlimited resources.
> —*Twyla Tharp in* The Creative Habit: Learn It and Use It for Life

Though the corporate world views a lack of resources as a difficult, if not insurmountable constraint, you've learned how, in this book, you can start your own business with limited capital. Beware the easy access to resources, because it can prevent you from developing your business as strongly as possible. Excess funds, even in small amounts, can encourage habits that make you less creative, less innovative, and less determined. In fact, the *New York Times* reports that there is now a substantial debate among economists as to whether providing developing countries with substantial aid actually hinders their long-term growth by encouraging inefficient practices. In this regard, countries and businesses are no different.

Many of the most successful companies are launched during difficult recessionary periods—precisely because they could succeed only through an innovative, highly disciplined approach to business. If you can launch the business and profitably attract customers with a bare minimum of resources, your likelihood of long-term success is high. You have demonstrated that you can handle anything. You have figured out how to create value while maintaining a low cost base, so your pricing is bound to be attractive. In addition, your low cost base almost certainly gives you great flexibility to adjust to changes in the marketplace. And, of critical importance, you are not dependent on anyone for additional funds. You have proven that you can go-it-alone.

THE WEB SITE FOR THIS BOOK

The Web site for this book has been designed to continue the mission of this book: to assist you in building a go-it-alone business. You are strongly encouraged to visit www.BruceJudson.com and investigate the wealth of resources:

- **An area where you can submit questions to me.** Although I may not be able to answer every question, I will do my best to post answers to questions that will be of interest to many readers.
- **A list of my favorite ASP resources for launching go-it-alone businesses.** I have assembled a substantial set of resources that will allow you to follow the advice in this book—to set up the infrastructure for your own business with just a small monthly investment. This substantial resource will be continuously updated.
- **Links to the latest news articles of interest to go-it-alone entrepreneurs.** I am constantly researching business trends, so I plan to share what I find with the book community.
- **The opportunity to sign up for the *Go-It-Alone!* newsletter.** As items and issues of interest to go-it-alone entrepreneurs arise, I will use the newsletter to let you know about them.
- **A place to submit your own story.** If you are interested in sharing your story with other entrepreneurs, here's your chance.

RESOURCES FOR GETTING STARTED

Note: The Web site for this book, www.BruceJudson.com, includes a more extensive list of valuable services, updated selections, and explanations of cutting-edge featured services that are particularly valuable for go-it-alone entrepreneurs. *Because Web-based services are constantly changing, I strongly encourage you to visit my Web site for this complete, up-to-date list of recommended services.*

A SAMPLING OF VALUABLE SERVICES FOR GO-IT-ALONE ENTREPRENEURS*

Insurance for Self-Employed Individuals

Individual and family health insurance: Health Plans Today (www.healthplanstoday.com)

Term life insurance: Life Insurance Anywhere (http://Term.LifeInsuranceAnywhere.com)

Disability coverage for self-employed individuals: (http://Disability.InsuranceAnywhere.net)

Business liability insurance: (http://Liability.InsuranceAnywhere.net)

---

*Full disclosure note: In a number of cases, I have a financial interest in the services listed on these pages. However, these business initiatives reflect the quality lesson discussed on page 163. I am involved only with services that I believe offer the *highest quality* to customers.

Business Establishment and Infrastructure

Unlimited phone calls throughout the U.S. for a flat monthly fee: Vonage (www.Vonage.com)

Trademark searches and applications: Mr. Trademark (www.MrTrademark.com)

Forming a corporation or LLC: Incorporate Anywhere (www.IncorporateAnywhere.net)

Logo design: 1800MYLOGO (www.1800mylogo.com)

Business cards and stationery: iPrint (www.iPrint.com)

Business DSL and broadband comparison shop: T1 Anywhere (www.T1Anywhere.com)

Comparison site for wireless phone plans: GetConnected (http://www.GetConnected.com)

For Computers and Related Equipment

Automated online data backup: @Backup (www.backup.com)

Phone technical support for hardware and software problems: *(See our Web site)*

Desktop e-mail and document management: Document Locater (www.DocumentLocater.com)

Discount and refurbished computer equipment: Overstock.com (www.Overstock.com)

Operating Your Business

Web-based project management and collaboration: iTeamwork (www.iTeamwork.com)

Secure extranet sharing projects with clients: WorkZone (www.myWorkZone.com)

Online surveys with analysis tools: Zoomerang
(www.Zoomerang.com)

Online sales presentations and Web conferencing: Webex
(www.Webex.com) and Raindance (www.Raindance.com)

Web-based sales management systems and CRM systems:
Salesnet.com (www.Salesnet.com) and Siebel CRM OnDemand
(www.CRMOnDemand.com)

Online database management and collaboration: Quickbase
(https://www.Quickbase.com)

Business research: HighBeam (www.HighBeam.com)

Online business accounting: QuickBooks Online edition
(http://oe.Quickbooks.com/home)

Management of recurring billing: Sapienter
(www.Sapienter.com)

Integrated inventory management, fulfillment management,
payment processing, and more: OrderMotion
(www.ordermotion.com)

Total integrated business management system: Netsuite
(www.NetSuite.com)

Creating and Operating Your Web Site

Easy-to-build Web site with e-commerce capabilities:
Yahoo! Merchant Solutions
(http://SmallBusiness.Yahoo.com/bzinfo/prod/com)

Easy-to-create Web site graphics: Xara Online
(www.XaraOnline.com)

E-mail list management: MailerMailer (with newsletter
creation tools) (www.MailerMailer.com) and Jango Mail
(for larger lists) (www.JangoMail.com)

Response forms for your Web site: SiteMason
(www.SiteMason.com)

Database query and response for your Web site: Caspio Bridge
(www.Caspio.com)

Web site traffic monitoring and analysis: HitBox Pro
(www.HitBoxPro.com)

Generate ad revenues from your Web site content
(if appropriate): Google AdSense (www.Google.com/AdSense)

Targeted marketing via selected pay-for-performance search
engines: Google AdWords (www.Google.com/AdWords) and
Overture Precision Match (www.Overture.com)

Special Articles and Listings Available at Our Web Site (www.BruceJudson.com)

1. New ASP resources for the go-it-alone entrepreneur

2. Sites and services that assist eBay merchants

3. How to profit from targeted pay-for-performance advertising

4. Overview of resources for serch engine optimization

BIBLIOGRAPHY

Allen, David, *Getting Things Done: The Art of Stress-Free Productivity.* Viking Penguin, 2001

Allen, David, *Ready for Anything: 52 Productivity Principles for Work & Life.* Viking Penguin, 2003

Allen, Robert G., *Multiple Streams of Income: How to Generate a Lifetime of Unlimited Wealth*, 2nd ed. John Wiley, 2004

Allen, Robert G., *Multiple Streams of Internet Income: How Ordinary People Make Extraordinary Money Online.* John Wiley, 2001

Barber, Brace E., *No Excuse Leadership: Lessons from the U.S. Army's Elite Rangers.* John Wiley, 2004

Boldt, Laurence G., *How to Find the Work You Love*, revised ed. Penguin Compass, 2004

Bossidy, Larry, and Charan, Ram, *Execution: The Discipline of Getting Things Done.* Crown Business, 2002

Bruch, Heike, and Ghoshal, Sumantra, *A Bias for Action: How Effective Managers Harness Their Willpower, Achieve Results, and Stop Wasting Time.* Harvard Business, 2004

Buckingham, Marcus, and Clifton, Donald, *Now, Discover Your Strengths.* Free Press, 2001

Canfield, Jack; Hansen, Mark Victor; and Hewitt, Les, *The Power of Focus: How to Hit Your Business, Personal and Financial Targets with Absolute Certainty.* Health Communications, 2000

Carnegie, Dale, *How to Stop Worrying and Start Living.* Pocket Books, 1985

Citrin, James M., and Smith, Richard A., *The 5 Patterns of Extraordinary Careers: The Guide for Achieving Success and Satisfaction.* Crown Business, 2003

Charan, Ram, *Profitable Growth Is Everyone's Business: 10 Tools You Can Use Monday Morning.* Crown Business, 2004

Christensen, Clayton M., *The Innovator's Dilemma: When New Technologies Cause Great Firms to Fail.* HarperBusiness, 2000

Christensen, Clayton M., and Raynor, Michael E., *The Innovator's Solution: Creating and Sustaining Successful Growth.* Harvard Business, 2003

Collins, Jim, *Good to Great: Why Some Companies Make the Leap . . . and Others Don't.* HarperBusiness, 2001

Collins, Jim, and Porras, Jerry I., *Built to Last: Successful Habits of Visionary Companies.* HarperBusiness Essentials, 2002

Corcoran, Barbara, with Littlefield, Bruce, *Use What You've Got; and Other Business Lessons I Learned from My Mom.* Portfolio, 2003

Dell, Michael, with Fredman, Catherine, *Direct from Dell: Strategies That Revolutionized an Industry.* HarperBusiness, 2000

DeLuca, Fred, with John P. Hayes, *Start Small, Finish Big: Fifteen Key Lessons to Start—and Run—Your Own Successful Business,* Warner, 2001

Drucker, David P., and Bruckenstein, Joel P., *Virtual Office Tools for a High-Margin Practice: How Client-Centered Financial dvisors Can Cut Paperwork, Overhead, and Wasted Hours.* Bloomberg, 2002

Drucker, Peter F., *The Essential Drucker: The Best of Sixty Years of Peter Drucker's Essential Writings on Management.* HarperBusiness, 2001

Finkelstein, Sydney, *Why Smart Executives Fail: And What You Can Learn from Their Mistakes.* Portfolio, 2003

Franklin, Benjamin, *The Autobiography of Benjamin Franklin.* Barnes & Noble, 1994

Gerber, Michael, E., *The E-Myth Contractor: Why Most Contractors' Businesses Don't Work and What to Do About It.* HarperBusiness, 2003

Gerber, Michael E., *The E-Myth Revisited: Why Most Small Businesses Don't Work and What to Do About It.* HarperBusiness, 2001

Gerstner, Jr., Louis V., *Who Says Elephants Can't Dance?: Leading a Great Enterprise Through Dramatic Change.* HarperBusiness, 2003

Girard, Joe, with Casemore, Robert, *How to Sell Yourself.* Warner, 2003

Gladwell, Malcolm, *The Tipping Point: How Little Things Can Make a Big Difference.* Little, Brown, 2000

Grove, Andrew S., *Only the Paranoid Survive: How to Exploit the Crisis Points That Challenge Every Company.* Doubleday, 1999

Hagel III, John, *Out of the Box: Strategies for Achieving Profits Today and Growth Tomorrow Through Web Services.* Harvard Business, 2002

Hall, Kathleen, *Alter Your Life: How to Turn Everyday Activities into Spiritually Rewarding Experiences*. Oak Haven, 2003

Hamel, Gary, *Leading the Revolution: How to Thrive in Turbulent Times by Making Innovation a Way of Life*. Plume, 2002

Hamel, Gary, and Prahalad, C. K., *Competing for the Future*. Harvard Business, 1996

Hammer, Michael, and Champy, James, *Reengineering the Corporation: A Manifesto for Business Revolution*, revised ed. HarperBusiness, 2001

Handy, Charles, *The Elephant and the Flea; Reflections of a Reluctant Capitalist*. Harvard Business, 2003

Isaacson, Walter, *Benjamin Franklin: An American Life*. Simon & Schuster, 2003

Jeffers, Susan, *Feel the Fear . . . and Beyond: Mastering the Techniques for Doing It Anyway*. Ballantine, 1998

Jeffers, Susan, *Feel the Fear and Do It Anyway*. Ballantine, 1988

Jennings, Jason, *Less Is More: How Great Companies Use Productivity as a Competitive Tool in Business*. Portfolio, 2002

Jennings, Jason, and Haughton, Laurence, *It's Not the Big That Eat the Small . . . It's the Fast That Eat the Slow: How to Use Speed as a Competitive Tool in Business*. HarperBusiness, 2002

Goodwin, Doris Kearns, *No Ordinary Time: Franklin and Eleanor Roosevelt: The Home Front in World War II*. Touchstone, 1995

Koch, Richard, *The 80/20 Individual: How to Accomplish More by Doing Less—The Nine Essentials of 80/20 Success at Work*. Currency, 2003

Koch, Richard, *The 80/20 Principle: The Secret to Success by Achieving More with Less*. Currency, 1998

Loehr, Jim, and Schwartz, Tony, *The Power of Full Engagement: Managing Energy, Not Time, Is the Key to High Performance and Personal Renewal*. Free Press, 2003

Malone, Thomas W., *The Future of Work: How the New Order of Business Will Shape Your Organization, Your Management Style, and Your Life*. Harvard Business, 2004

Manchester, William, *The Last Lion: Winston Spencer Churchill: Alone, 1932-1940*. Delta, 1984

Maxwell, John C., *Failing Forward: Turning Mistakes into Stepping Stones for Success*. Thomas Nelson, 2000

Maxwell, John C., *Thinking for a Change: 11 Ways Highly Successful People Approach Life and Work*. Warner, 2003

McCullough, David, *The Great Bridge: The Epic Story of the Building of the Brooklyn Bridge*. Simon & Schuster, 1983

Meachum, Jon, *Franklin & Winston: An Intimate Portrait of an Epic Friendship*, Random House, 2003

Nalebuff, Barry, and Ayres, Ian, *Why Not? How to Use Everyday Ingenuity to Solve Problems Big and Small*. Harvard Business, 2003

Pink, Daniel, H., *Free Agent Nation: The Future of Working for Yourself*. Warner, 2002

Prahalad, C. K., and Ramaswamy, Venkat, *The Future of Competition: Co-Creating Unique Value with Customers*. Harvard Business, 2004

Ries, Al, *Focus: The Future of Your Company Depends on It*. Harper-Business, 1997

Ries, Al, and Trout, Jack, *Marketing Warfare*. McGraw-Hill, 1997

Ries , Al, and Trout, Jack, *The 22 Immutable Laws of Marketing: Violate Them at Your Own Risk!* HarperBusiness, 1994

Rhodes, Richard, *The Making of the Atomic Bomb*. Simon & Schuster, 1986

Robinson, Allen G., and Schroeder, Dean M., *Ideas Are Free: How the Idea Revolution Is Liberating People and Transforming Organizations*. Berrett-Koehler, 2004

Rubin, Ron, and Gold, Stuart Avery, *Tiger Heart, Tiger Mind: How to Empower Your Dream*. Newmarket, 2004

Schwartz, Peter, *Inevitable Surprises: Thinking Ahead in a Time of Turbulence*. Gotham, 2003

Slywotzky, Adrian, and Wise, Richard, with Weber, Karl, *How to Grow When Markets Don't*. Warner, 2003

Slywotzky, Adrian J., and Morrison, David J., with Andelman, Bob, *The Profit Zone: How Strategic Business Design Will Lead You to Tomorrow's Profits*. Three Rivers, 2002

Tharp, Twyla, *The Creative Habit: Learn It and Use It for Life*. Simon & Schuster, 2003

Trout, Jack, with Rivkin, Steve, *The Power of Simplicity: A Management Guide to Cutting Through the Nonsense and Doing Things Right*. McGraw-Hill, 1999

Welch, Jack, with Byrne, John A., *Jack: Straight from the Gut*. Warner, 2001

Zook, Chris, *Beyond the Core: Expand Your Markets Without Abandoning Your Roots*. Harvard Business, 2004

Zook, Chris, with Allen, James, *Profit from the Core: Growth Strategy in an Era of Turbulence*. Harvard Business, 2001

INDEX